GEOGRAPHY AND HISTORY SECONDARY

BY ME

TERRITORY, POPULATION AND URBANISATION

Cristina Granda Gallego
Raúl Núñez Heras
José María Segoviano
Andrew Critchley

Contents

01 Territorial divisions

<< LOOKING BACK

- What is democracy? What is the difference between democratic countries and authoritarian regimes?
- What are the geographical boundaries between Europe and Asia?
- How many state members does the European Union have?
- Where is the European Parliament based?
- What is the UN? What are its main objectives?
- When was the Spanish Constitution ratified?

The brutal Draconian laws

'Citizens of Greece! This is a wonderful day, because for the first time we have true justice!

Before today only the rich people knew all our laws, and they changed the rules depending on who was breaking them. Now, thanks to our kind and benevolent Draco, all the laws of the land are displayed in public so everyone can know them (as long as they can read, like the rich people).

Naturally, there must be punishments. Anyone who owes money and cannot pay will be sold into slavery (unless they are from the upper classes, of course). And from now on, the standard penalty will be DEATH – whether you committed a murder or just stole a cabbage!

Thousands of years from now, people will look back on the draconian democracy of Ancient Greece and say, *Never has there been a more fair and equal society!'*

- Who was Draco? When did he live? What did he do?
- The speechwriter thinks that Draconian laws are very moderate and fair. Is he right?
- Does the speechwriter really think that Draco is benevolent? Why or why not?
- Draconian laws played an important role in the growth of democracy in Athens. Do you think his laws were democratic? Is modern democracy similar to this one initiated in Athens?
- How has criminal justice changed since Draco's time?

LOOKING FORWARD >>

- Is Spain a monarchy or a republic?
- What does 'UN' stand for?
- How many countries are there in Europe? And in the EU?
- What is a parliamentary monarchy?

1 Political and territorial divisions

Is Spain a monarchy or a republic?

1.1 States

Today's societies are organised in **political** and **legal units** called states. Each state has the following:

- Its own **territory**, the area over which the state exercises its authority. Each territory is defined by internationally recognised **borders** and includes land, sea, airspace and the subsoil.
- A **population** living in the territory. The inhabitants of a state are its **citizens**, i.e., they are bound by its laws and beneficiaries of the rights guaranteed by those laws.
- Sovereign and independent **power**, i.e., the ability to pass laws and govern itself both inside its borders and in international relations with other countries. States create a series of government and judicial institutions to administer that power.

THE WORLD'S STATES

There are currently around 200 states in the world's five inhabited continents.

Each state has its own symbols: a national anthem, flag and coat of arms.

1.2 Types of state

Although all states share the characteristics above, they also have different types of government. States can be classified according to their system of government.

ACCORDING TO THE HEAD OF STATE

The **head of state** is the state's chief public representative. There are two types of states according to who the head of state is:

- **Monarchies**. The head of state is a king or a queen. The title is hereditary.
- **Republics**. The head of state is a president.

ACCORDING TO THE WAY IN WHICH THE TERRITORY IS DIVIDED

The internal organisation of states can also vary:

- **Decentralised states**. Some territories within the state have a certain degree of autonomy, but they share administrative responsibilities and some common laws with the central government. Federal states and countries with autonomous regions are examples of decentralised states.
- **Centralised states**. The central government is the only administration.

PUBLIC ADMINISTRATION

The public administration is the set of state institutions responsible for public affairs: ministries, councils, autonomous regions, etc.

The employees of these bodies are called civil servants.

Ministry of Agriculture *(Ministerio de Agricultura)* headquarters in Madrid

ACTIVITIES

1. List the elements that define a state.
2. Is Spain a decentralised state or centralised state?
3. Search for information about monarchies and republics. How are they different? Find three examples of each. Locate them on a world map.
4. Find two examples of decentralised states and centralised states.

ACCORDING TO THE DISTRIBUTION OF POWER

The state's **three fundamental powers** can be separate (in a **democracy**) or controlled by one person (in a **dictatorship**).

Legislative power
Makes laws.

Executive power
Governs the country.

Judicial power
Ensures that laws are enforced.

1.3 Characteristics of democratic states

SEPARATION OF POWERS

The three fundamental powers are held by different people or institutions:

- **Legislative power**. The parliament drafts and approves laws.
- **Executive power**. The government governs in accordance with the laws approved by the parliament.
- **Judicial power**. The courts of justice make sure that laws are enforced.

UNIVERSAL SUFFRAGE

National sovereignty is exercised through the **right to vote** in free elections. These elections are used to choose parliamentary representatives and the government. Candidates run for election in different political parties.

The election is held in accordance with universal suffrage, the right of all citizens to vote in elections without discrimination.

RULE OF LAW

Democratic states are governed by the rule of **law**. States are constitutional and governed by the rule of law when a fundamental law or **constitution** is established. This law sets out the basic rules by which the state will function and the rights and duties of its citizens.

NATIONAL SOVEREIGNTY

Sovereignty is the **supreme power** or authority within a territory. Thanks to national sovereignty, citizens can decide how they want to be organised and choose who will govern them.

1.4 Characteristics of dictatorships

Dictatorships are **authoritarian regimes** where there is no separation of powers and citizens cannot choose leaders. All three fundamental powers of state are held by the government. Human rights are not respected, freedom of expression and assembly is restricted, and citizens cannot criticise the regime.

ACTIVITIES

5. What are the differences between democratic states and authoritarian regimes?
6. What is universal suffrage?
7. Do you know any authoritarian regimes? Identify them on a world map.

2 Supranational organisations

What does 'UN' stand for?

Groups of states come together to form supranational institutions so that they can cooperate in order to prevent conflict, improve education, protect cultural heritage and promote development.

2.1 The United Nations (UN)

The UN is the most important supranational organisation because almost all internationally recognised states are members. It was **formed in 1945**, after the Second World War. Its **purposes** are set out in the Charter of the United Nations:

- To **maintain** international **peace** and **security**.
- To develop friendly relations among **nations** based on respect for the principle of **equal rights**.
- To achieve **international cooperation** in **solving international problems** of an economic, social, cultural or humanitarian character, and in promoting respect for **fundamental freedoms**.
- To be a centre for **harmonising the actions** of nations in the attainment of these common goals.

The UN headquarters are in New York

THE UN STRUCTURE

GENERAL ASSEMBLY

All UN member states are represented in the General Assembly and they all have the right to vote. The General Assembly approves **budgets**, initiates studies to promote cooperation and selects the members of other UN organs.

SECURITY COUNCIL

The Security Council is responsible for maintaining international peace. It has five permanent members: the United States, the United Kingdom, France, China and Russia. There are also 10 non-permanent members elected every two years by the General Assembly. However, only the five permanent members have the right to **veto**, i.e., the ability to stop a decision being made. Although the General Assembly makes recommendations to the Security Council, it is the Security Council that makes decisions about conflict mediation, deploying UN peacekeepers or **imposing** economic sanctions on countries that do not comply with international law.

SECRETARY-GENERAL

This is the UN's leader and **spokesperson**. The Secretary-General is elected by the General Assembly every five years.

BLUE HELMETS

UN peacekeepers are soldiers from UN member states. They are known as 'Blue Helmets'. They operate on the basis of mandates from the UN Security Council.

ACTIVITIES

8. When was the United Nations created?
9. What are the main objectives of the UN?
10. Which member countries of the UN can stop a decision being made?

UN ORGANISATIONS

To meet its economic, social, cultural and judicial objectives, the UN has various specialised agencies and organisations.

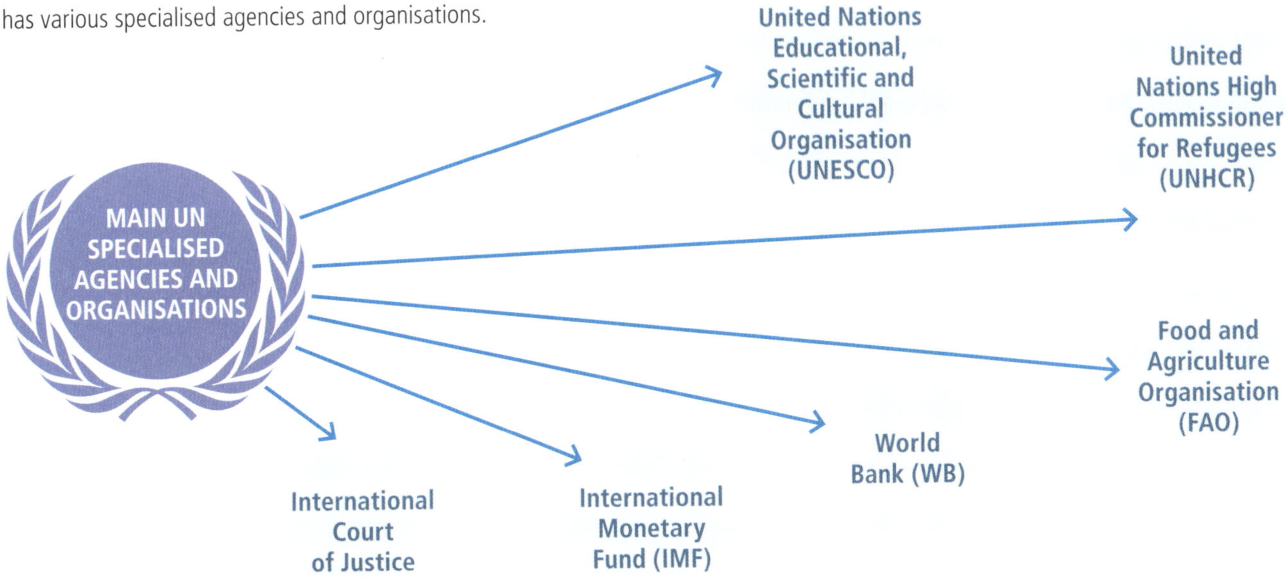

2.2 Other supranational organisations

In addition to the UN, there are other supranational organisations that have been established to achieve specific objectives.

ECONOMIC

The most important ones are:

- The **Organisation for Economic Co-operation and Development (OECD)**. It aims to promote employment and economic growth.
- The **World Trade Organisation (WTO)**. It aims to stimulate trade relationships.

POLITICAL

A number of organisations aim to promote development and cooperation between similar countries in a region.

Examples include the **African Union**, the **Arab League**, the **Organisation of Ibero-American States** and the **European Union**.

MILITARY

The **North Atlantic Treaty Organisation (NATO)** was established in 1949 because of political tension between the United States and the Soviet Union after the Second World War.

NATO is currently responsible for protecting the security of its member countries.

2.3 Non-governmental organisations (NGOs)

In addition to government-dependent supranational organisations, a number of independent non-governmental organisations were founded in the 20th century. These social movements aim to alleviate problems related to human rights, poverty or disease. Many NGOs have voluntary staff and are funded by private donations from members and institutions.

The largest NGOs are international, i.e., various states are members. Examples include the Red Cross and Doctors Without Borders.

ACTIVITIES

11. What economic organisations depend on the UN?

12. What other NGOs do you know? What do they do?

3 Territorial divisions in Europe

How many countries are there in Europe? And in the EU?

3.1 Countries in Europe

Europe, along with Asia, is part of the continental land mass of Eurasia. Europe and Asia are separated by the Ural Mountains. Europe consists of a large number of different states.

- There are **50 states** in Europe. However, this number is not accepted by all of the international community. Some states are not recognised by all countries and others are considered to be part of Asia.
- The **areas** of the different European **states** vary widely. The largest country in the world, Russia, and some of the smallest, such as Monaco and Vatican City, are in Europe.
- Europe has an **area** of approximately 10.5 square million kilometres, although this figure can vary depending on whether you count the territories that European states have in other continents.
- The **borders** of European states have changed a lot throughout history. Even today, there are diplomatic tensions between countries because of the locations of the borders of some states.

Democracy is the **system of government** in most European states. However, there are many different types of systems:

- There are **monarchies**, such as the United Kingdom, and **republics**, such as Greece.
- Some states, such as France, have a **centralised government**, and others, such as Germany, have a **federal government**.

3.2 The European Union

One of the most important regional **supranational organisations** to have been founded in Europe is the European Union (EU). It was established after the Second World War to promote **economic cooperation**. Since then, there have been several enlargements and agreements signed to promote political integration, and the EU now has **28 member states** working together to implement common policies.

ACTIVITIES

13. What type of government exists in the UK, France, Germany and Greece?
14. What policies does the European Union promote?
15. Identify the boundary between Europe and Asia.
16. Why have the borders of European states changed so much? Give examples.

EU member countries and date joined	
Belgium, the Netherlands, Luxembourg, Germany, Italy, France	1957
Ireland, the United Kingdom, Denmark	1973
Greece	1981
Spain, Portugal	1986
Austria, Sweden, Finland	1995
Estonia, Latvia, Lithuania, Poland, Hungary, Czech Republic, Slovakia, Slovenia, Malta, Cyprus	2004
Bulgaria, Romania	2007
Croatia	2013

BIG THINKER

Paul-Henri Spaak was the first President of the United Nations General Assembly. During the First World War, he lied about his age so he could join the army. In the Second World War, he escaped from the Nazis by hiding in a truck to Portugal. Spaak also played tennis for Belgium in the 1922 Davis Cup! Do you know any other politicians with sporting backgrounds?

3.3 Main European Union institutions

EUROPEAN COUNCIL

Formed by the heads of state or government of the 28 member states. It meets several times a year to define the EU's general political direction.

Europa building in Brussels

COUNCIL OF THE EU

Formed by government ministers from the 28 member states. It is the EU's main legislative body. It coordinates foreign economic policy and is also responsible for security matters.

EU Council headquarters in Brussels

EUROPEAN PARLIAMENT

Members of the European Parliament, representing all member states, are elected by universal suffrage every five years. The Parliament approves the EU budget and laws proposed by the Council.

European Parliament building in Strasbourg

EUROPEAN COMMISSION

The EU's executive body. It is formed by 28 commissioners, one for each member state. It proposes legislation to the EU council and implements European policies.

European Commission building in Brussels

ACTIVITIES

17. What is the European Parliament's function?

18. How many members compose the European Commission?

4 The Spanish state

What is a parliamentary monarchy?

4.1 The Spanish Constitution of 1978

Spain is a **social** and **democratic** state governed by the **rule of law**. Its territories are organised in accordance with its **Constitution**. The Constitution is the set of fundamental principles by which Spain is governed. It was ratified by a referendum of the Spanish people in 1978 and sets out the rights and duties of Spanish citizens. According to the Constitution, Spain is established as:

- A **kingdom**, although national **sovereignty** belongs to the Spanish people, not to the monarch.
- A **democratic state** subject to the **rule of law**, with **separation of powers** and representatives freely elected by **universal suffrage**.
- A **territorially decentralised** state.
- A **constitutional or parliamentary monarchy** (both a kingdom and a democratic state). A constitutional monarchy is a monarchical political system where the monarch is the head of state but sovereignty belongs to the people. The monarchs therefore do not intervene in government, legislation or administration of justice.

THE SPANISH MONARCHY

The King of Spain is currently Felipe VI. His functions and responsibilities are set out in the Constitution:

- He is the representative of the state.
- The post of king is held for life, i.e., it lasts as long as the king lives or until he renounces the throne to his successor (abdication).
- It is a hereditary title, i.e., it is passed down from parents to their children. According to the Constitution, the title is **inherited** by the monarch's eldest son, the Prince of Asturias.
- Felipe VI became king in 2014 after his father Juan Carlos I abdicated. Because Felipe has no sons, his daughter Leonor, Princess of Asturias, will inherit the throne.

HISTORY OF THE SPANISH STATE

3rd century BC

The Iberian Peninsula was incorporated into the Roman Empire: the first period of political, administrative and religious unity.

6th century

Visigothic Kingdom of Toledo: inherited the Roman method of organisation and established new territorial divisions.

8th century

For a large part of the Middle Ages, there were many changes to the borders of the peninsula's kingdoms because of the Muslim presence.

13th century

The Peninsula was divided into five kingdoms: the Kingdom of Portugal, the Kingdom of Navarra, the Crown of Aragón, the Crown of Castilla and the Kingdom of Granada.

15th century

The Catholic Monarchs brought together the Crowns of Aragón and Castilla and annexed the Kingdoms of Granada and Navarra.

Early Modern Period: the Habsburg monarchs maintained the dynastic union, i.e., each kingdom kept its own laws and institutions.

18th century

Arrival of the Bourbons in 1700: new centralist policies and territorial uniformisation.

19th century

Spain was divided into provinces and regions.

20th century

The Constitution of 1978 established a decentralised state with Autonomous Communities.

4.2 Central administration

The term 'central administration' refers to the institutions whose powers extend throughout all of Spain's territorial divisions. Central administrative bodies are based in the state capital, Madrid.

According to the Constitution, Spain is a state with separation of powers. Therefore, each of the fundamental powers of state are held by different institutions.

LEGISLATIVE POWER

In Spain, laws are written by the **Parliament *(Cortes Generales)***. It is a bicameral institution, i.e., it has two chambers of representatives, the **Congress of Deputies *(Congreso de los Diputados)*** and the **Senate *(Senado)***.

There are two types of Parliament members: deputies *(diputados)* and senators *(senadores)*. These **representatives** are directly elected by the people in the **general election** every four years by universal suffrage. Everyone's vote is secret. All Spanish citizens over 18 years of age, men and women, can vote or be voted for in elections. Members of Parliament work together in groups called **political parties**.

Congress of Deputies building and Senate building

EXECUTIVE POWER

This branch is responsible for governing in accordance with the laws drafted and approved by the Parliament. The **Government *(Gobierno)*** can also propose new laws for approval. The Government consists of the **Prime Minister *(Presidente del Gobierno)*** and other **ministers**. The Prime Minister has to be **sworn** in by the Parliament, so usually belongs to the political party with a parliamentary majority. Ministers are heads of different ministries: education and culture, development, justice, defence, finance, etc.

Adolfo Suárez

JUDICIAL POWER

This branch ensures that all public and private activities are done in accordance with the law. We turn to this power when we believe that a crime has been committed or that our legal rights have not been respected.

The **courts** are responsible for imparting justice. The most important court is the **Supreme Court *(Tribunal Supremo)***. However, there are other courts with specific powers: the **Constitutional Court *(Tribunal Constitucional)***, which ensures that the Constitution is being upheld, and the **National Court *(Audiencia Nacional)***, which deals with crimes related to state security.

Constitutional Court building

ACTIVITIES

19. The Constitution signed in 1978 is not the first Constitution in the Spanish history. Find out more about the first Constitution and answer the questions:

a. When was it signed?

b. Where was it signed?

c. What principles did it establish?

20. What functions does the Congress have?

21. What is the Government's main responsibility?

22. When do people turn to judicial power?

23. What is the difference between the Supreme Court and the Constitutional Court?

4.3 Autonomous governments

Spain is divided into 17 **Autonomous Communities** and two **Autonomous Cities**. The Constitution of 1978 recognises the right to self-government of these Communities.

Each Autonomous Community has a **Statute of Autonomy** that defines how the Community is organised and which government matters it is responsible for: healthcare, education, etc. It also defines the territory, the capital city and the symbols of the Autonomous Community.

The Autonomous Communities hold elections every four years. An **Autonomous Parliament** is elected by universal suffrage. The **President** ***(Presidente)*** of the Autonomous Community, who governs together with his or her **Regional Ministers** ***(Consejeros)***, is also voted in.

4.4 Local governments

Autonomous Communities are divided into **provinces** formed of **municipalities**. There are 50 provinces in Spain.

LOCAL AND PROVINCIAL GOVERNMENT INSTITUTIONS

CITY COUNCILS *(AYUNTAMIENTOS)*

Municipalities are the smallest administrative units. Municipal governments are called **City Councils *(ayuntamientos)***. They are formed by **councillors *(concejales)*** under the leadership of the **mayor *(alcalde)***. The mayor and councillors are democratically elected every four years by residents of the municipality.

PROVINCIAL COUNCILS *(DIPUTACIONES PROVINCIALES)*

Provincial Councils are the governing bodies of Spain's provinces. Each one is led by a **Provincial Council President**, who is elected by all of the province's mayors. Provincial Councils are basically responsible for matters related to infrastructure and artistic and cultural heritage.

However, there are no Provincial Councils in Autonomous Communities with just one province, for example the Comunidad de Madrid. In these cases, the Autonomous Government is responsible for Provincial Council functions.

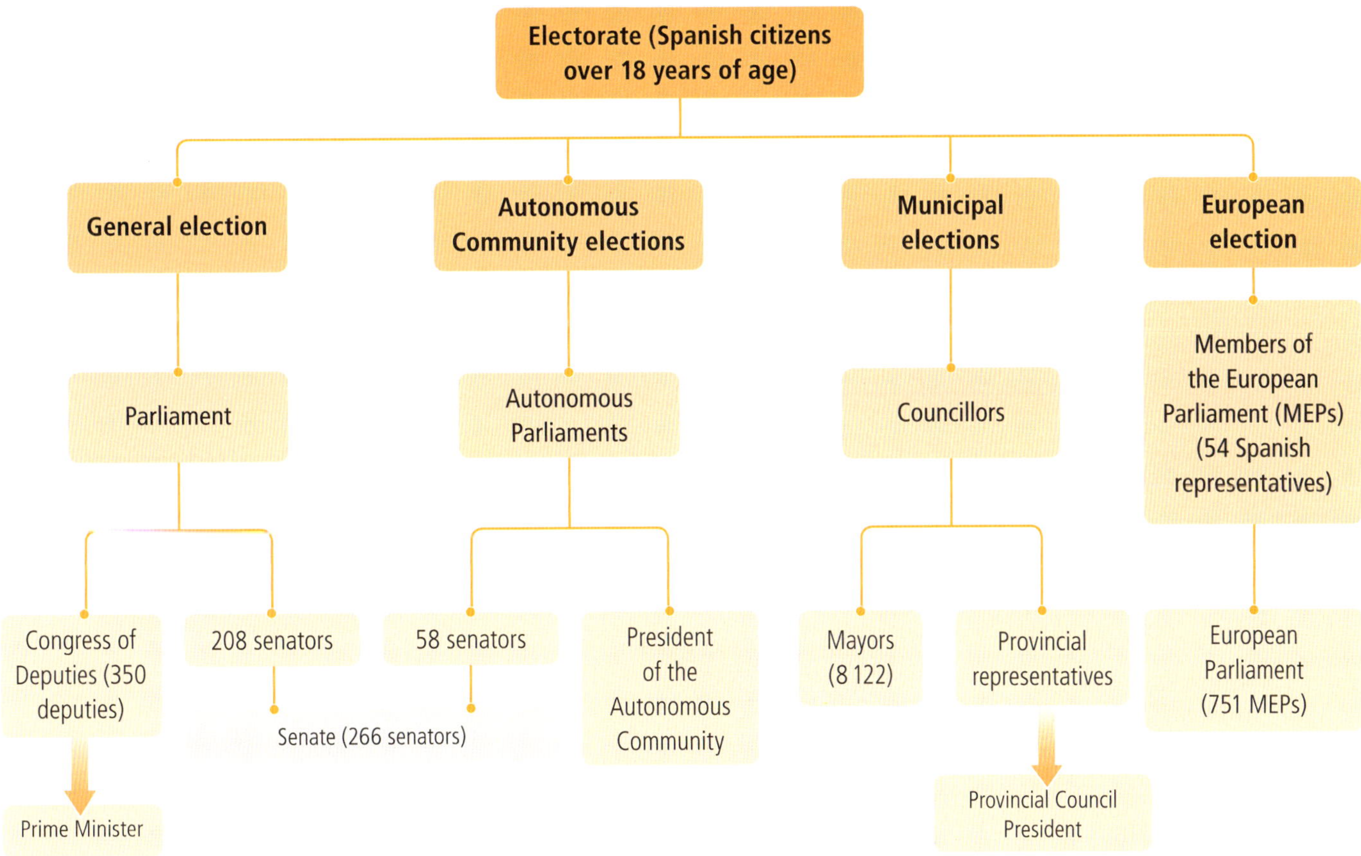

ACTIVITIES

24. How often do autonomous elections take place?

25. Who elects the Prime Minister?

26. Why can the number of senators change?

27. Do all the Autonomous Communities have Provincial Councils?

DID YOU KNOW?

The majority of senators (208) are elected directly by citizens. The rest of them are elected by the Autonomous Communities, depending on the population of each. This number can vary from 51 to 58.

Discovery techniques

ANALYSING AN ORGANISATION CHART

What are organisation charts?

Organisation charts are diagrams that show how institutions are structured and organised. They can be used for companies, football teams, ministries, etc.

They give a simple overview of highly complex structures at a glance. They also show the relationships between different ranks or departments. To analyse an organisation chart, follow the steps below.

How to analyse an organisation chart

1. OBSERVATION
The first step is to identify what the organisation chart represents and what symbols or techniques are being used to represent it: shapes, fonts, layout, lines, etc.

2. ANALYSIS
Now you can interpret the chart's meaning. You need to identify the ranks and hierarchy, i.e., the relationships between the different ranks/departments.

3. COMMENTARY
Finally, write a commentary explaining what the institution does and how it is organised. It would be interesting to explain why it is structured the way it is.

Below is an example analysing the organisation chart of the UN.

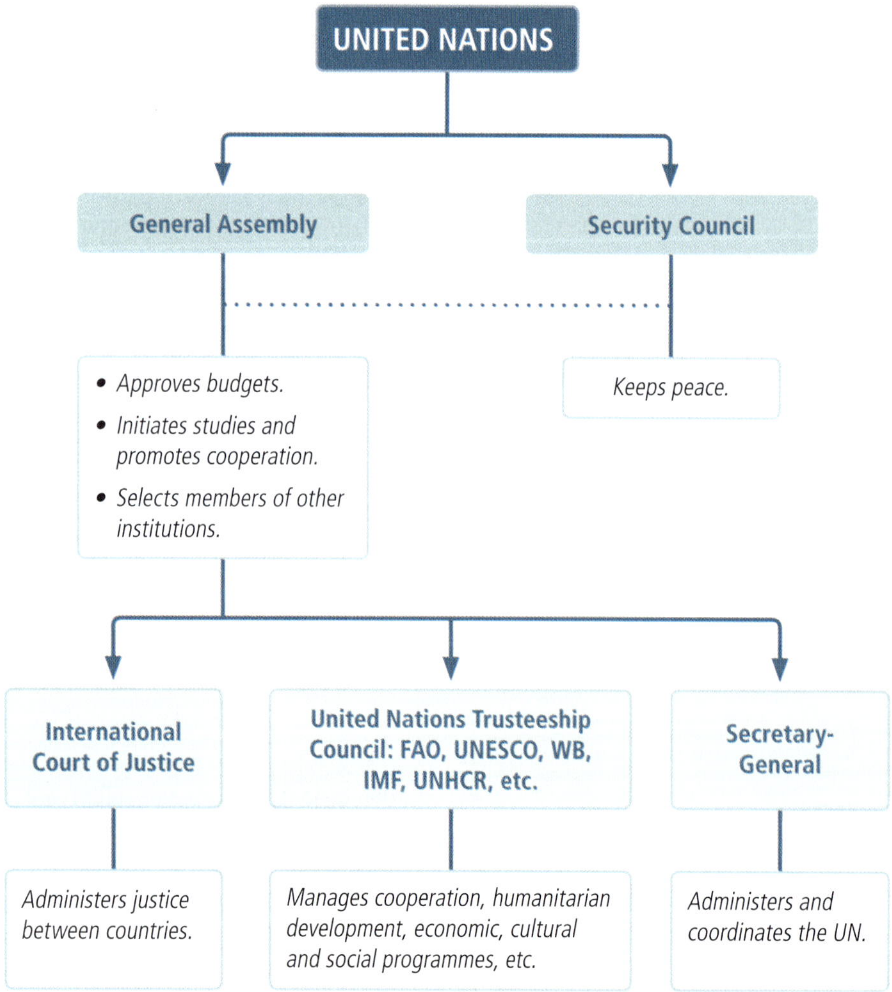

1. OBSERVATION

The organisation chart shows the different UN organs, their functions and the relationships between them.

The **symbols** and **techniques** used are:

- Different **fonts** and font sizes to differentiate between ranks.

  MAIN INSTITUTION

  Other organs

- **Colours** to differentiate between institutions and their functions.

  Institution | *Functions*

- **Layout.** The elements are organised from left to right and from top to bottom to make it easier to visualise the hierarchy.
- **Lines** joining the information:
  - → Direct dependence
  - — Indirect relationship
  - ...... Relationship between organ and function

Why are organisation charts useful?

2. ANALYSIS

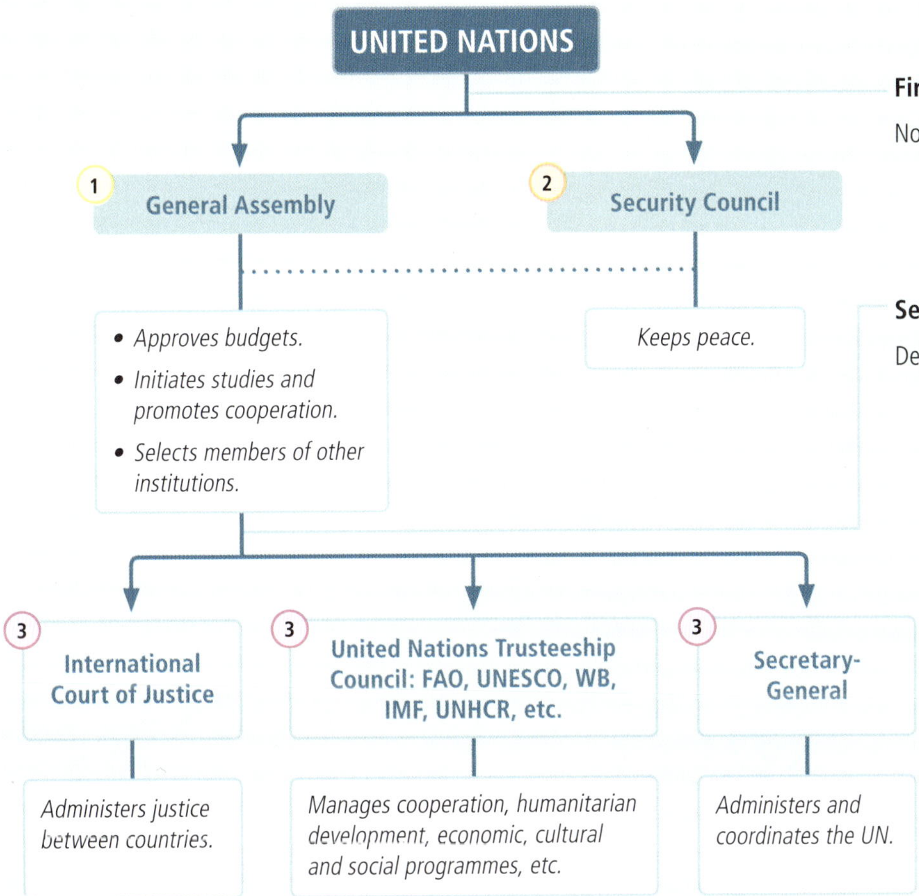

First rank.

Not dependent on other institutions.

Second rank.

Dependent on the General Assembly.

1. The most important organ because of the number of functions it has and because most institutions are dependent on it.
2. Responsible for keeping peace. To fulfil this function, the council's permanent members have the right to veto.
3. Responsible for managing various matters. They have the same level of importance in the UN hierarchy.

3. COMMENTARY

The UN is the most important supranational organisation and it has 193 member states. It is responsible for maintaining international peace and promoting cooperation and development.

Its role is so complex that it has to be organised into separate organs that are responsible for and specialise in different functions: the General Assembly, the Security Council, the International Court of Justice, etc.

It is also a hierarchical organisation, as the layout and format of the different organs in the organisation chart show. Only the Security Council's special decision-making powers in matters relating to peacekeeping, one of the main reasons the UN was founded, are not consistent with this hierarchical structure.

ACTIVITIES

1. Can the Security Council choose the members of the International Court of Justice? Who does?
2. Can the General Assembly decide to send UN peacekeepers to a conflict zone? What is the only thing it can do in these cases?
3. Visit the UN website (www.un.org) and find out the functions of the FAO, UNESCO, WB, IMF and UNHCR.

UN General Assembly hall

Revision activities

1. On an outline map like the one below:
   a. Identify the European countries.
   b. Identify the countries located on an island.
   c. Identify the countries with a Mediterranean coast.
   d. How many EU member countries are there? Identify them on the map.
   e. Identify the seas.
   f. Name the countries that border the following states:
      - Slovakia
      - Luxembourg
      - Switzerland
      - Germany
      - Belarus
      - Poland

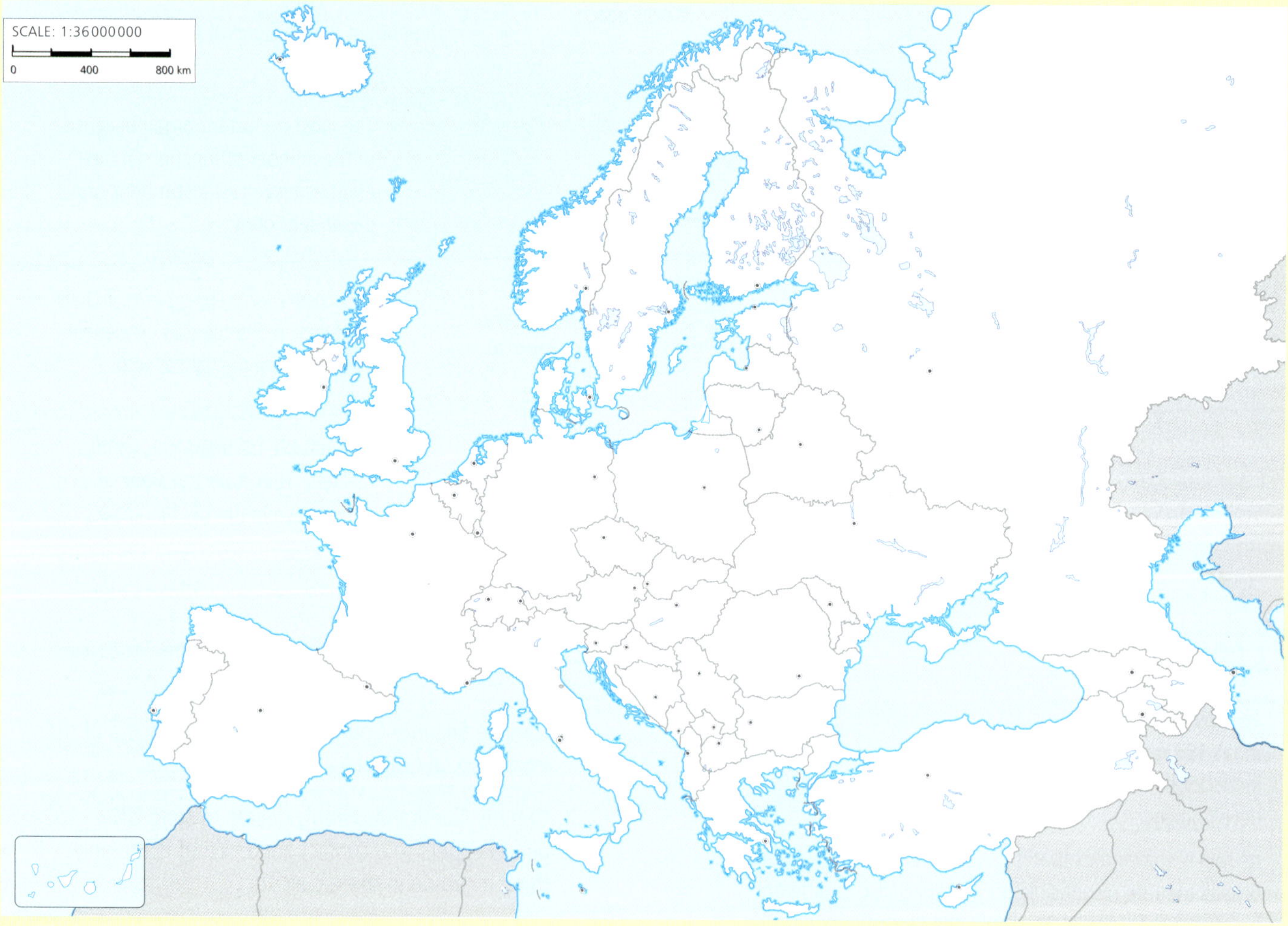

2. Explain how states are classified. Which categories does Spain belong to?

3. Think about the different types of supranational organisations in the world. To which category does the European Union belong? Which other institutions belong to this category?

4. Explain the following terms:
   - universal suffrage
   - national sovereignty
   - dictatorship
   - democracy
   - border

5 Read the preamble of the Spanish Constitution below. Answer the questions that follow.

> “The Spanish Nation, desiring to establish justice, liberty, and security, and to promote the well-being of all its members, in the exercise of its sovereignty, proclaims its will to:
>
> - Guarantee democratic coexistence within the Constitution and the laws, in accordance with a fair economic and social order.
> - Consolidate a state which ensures the rule of law as the expression of the popular will.
> - Protect all Spaniards and peoples of Spain in the exercise of human rights, of their culture and traditions, languages and institutions.
> - Promote the progress of culture and of the economy to ensure a dignified quality of life for all.
> - Establish an advanced democratic society.
> - Cooperate in the strengthening of peaceful relations and effective cooperation among all the peoples of the earth.
>
> Therefore, the Parliament passes and the Spanish people ratify the following Constitution.”

Source: *La Constitución española* (translated and adapted)

a. What are constitutions and what types of states are governed in accordance with them?
b. What does 'in the exercise of its sovereignty' mean in relation to the Spanish people?
c. What does it mean when a state is 'governed by the rule of law'?
d. Why is it important to respect the cultures, traditions and languages of peoples? How many languages are there in Spain?
e. The desire to cooperate in international relations is evident in Spain's involvement in various institutions. Name two international institutions of which Spain is a member.

6 What are the fundamental powers? What does it mean if a state has separation of powers? Describe the separation of powers in Spain, giving the name(s) of the institution(s) responsible for each one.

7 Describe two similarities and two differences between the Spanish Parliament and Government.

8 Investigate the name of the mayor of your city, the President of your Autonomous Community, the year when they were chosen and the political party they belong to.

9 Classify the following organisations.

NATO, OXFAM, UN, UNHCR, UNESCO, MERCOSUR, Red Cross, Red Crescent, Human Rights Watch, Amnesty International

International NGOs	Supranational organisations

10 Read the text and answer the questions below.

> “**The IMF at a Glance**
>
> The IMF, also known as the Fund, was conceived at a UN conference in Bretton Woods, New Hampshire, United States, in July 1944. The 44 countries at that conference sought to build a framework for economic cooperation to avoid a repetition of the competitive devaluations that had contributed to the Great Depression of the 1930s.
>
> The IMF's responsibilities: The IMF's primary purpose is to ensure the stability of the international monetary system—the system of exchange rates and international payments that enables countries (and their citizens) to transact with each other. The Fund's mandate was updated in 2012 to include all macroeconomic and financial sector issues that bear on global stability.
>
> The IMF's fundamental mission is to ensure the stability of the international monetary system. It does so in three ways: keeping track of the global economy and the economies of member countries; lending to countries with balance of payments difficulties; and giving practical help to members.”

Source: http://www.imf.org/external/about.htm

a. What was the IMF's original aim?
b. What changed in 2012?
c. What measures does the IMF take to reach its objectives?

Read and think

FROM WARFARE TO DIPLOMACY

The king of Aragón, Alfonso I, became known as *'el Batallador'*, and English kings William I and Richard I were nicknamed 'the Conqueror' and 'the Lionheart', respectively. These names give us a good idea of the main function of medieval monarchs: to wage war in order to acquire lands and wealth or to impose religious beliefs.

In the Middle Ages, the king and the barons were the most powerful people. The king owned all the land. However, as he could not control it all, he gave land to the barons, who controlled it, established their own tax laws and even printed their own money. The barons paid the king rent for the land, advised him and provided him with knights when he needed them.

With the discoveries of the Early Modern Age, some European monarchs became rulers of huge territories and began to believe that they had a 'divine right', i.e., God had given them absolute power to make all the decisions about their countries. For example, during the 72-year reign of Louis XIV of France, no decision was made about the nation without his approval. Absolutism declined in western Europe after the French Revolution in 1789, and absolute monarchies became constitutional monarchies or parliamentary republics.

Today, in Spain's constitutional monarchy, the king has very limited powers. He is the commander of the armed forces and he approves laws on the recommendation of the President or Parliament. However, like other European monarchs, he plays a very important role in international relations and represents Spain abroad. Probably preferable to going to war as some of his ancestors did!

William I

Louis XIV of France

ANSWER THE QUESTIONS

1. What do the nicknames *'Batallador'*, 'Conqueror' and 'Lionheart' suggest about the people they were given to? Find out more about William I and Richard I. Why were they given these nicknames?
2. Why did medieval monarchs often go to war?
3. Who helped medieval monarchs? How?
4. What did the barons give the monarch in exchange for land?
5. What is an absolute monarchy?
6. How long was Louis XIV king of France?
7. What was one of the reasons for the decline of absolutism in Europe?
8. What is a constitutional monarchy? Think about what you have learnt in the unit.
9. What are the main functions of the King of Spain today?
10. Investigate and discuss.
    a. Find a nation which still has an absolute monarch today. Note down the location of the nation, the name of the monarch and the powers he has.
    b. Explain your findings.
    c. Which type of monarch would you prefer to be? Why?

Work it out

CONCEPT MAP

Use the words in the word cloud to create your own unit map in your notebook. Write any connecting texts you need.

characteristics of democratic states
military
monarchy
centralised
WTO
republic
economic
territorial divisions
types of state
decentralised
UN
political
universal suffrage
NATO
rule of law
other supranational organisations
EU
dictatorship
separation of powers
democratic
national sovereignty

SELF-ASSESSMENT

Carry out a self-assessment of what you learnt in this unit. Choose one answer for each question and then check your answers.

1. Which of these characteristics does not define a democratic state?
   a. separation of powers
   b. national sovereignty
   c. lack of freedom of expression
2. Which of the following is the EU's executive body?
   a. the European Council
   b. the European Parliament
   c. the European Commission
3. Which institution has legislative power in Spain?
   a. the Parliament
   b. the Government
   c. the National Court
4. The way in which each Autonomous Community is organised is established in the ...
   a. Autonomous Constitution.
   b. Institute of Autonomy.
   c. Statute of Autonomy.
5. The smallest administrative units in Spain are governed by the ...
   a. Provincial Council President.
   b. Mayor.
   c. Senator.
6. Spain's head of state is ...
   a. the Prime Minister.
   b. the king.
   c. the Senate.
7. Which of these organisations has military objectives?
   a. OECD
   b. NATO
   c. EU
8. Which of these organisations is not a non-governmental organisation?
   a. Red Cross
   b. Doctors Without Borders
   c. WTO
9. How many member states does the EU have?
   a. 23
   b. 28
   c. 27
10. When did Spain join the EU?
    a. in 1986
    b. in 1968
    c. in 1998

02 Population

<< LOOKING BACK

- What is life expectancy?
- Is life expectancy similar in Europe and Africa? Why?
- Why do people migrate?
- Look at photos A and B. Why are some places more populated than others?
- Why has the world population increased so quickly over the last century?
- Look at photos C and D. What is overpopulation? What consequences can it have?

A

B

C

Forest migration

Everyone knows that a tree can't move from the place it grows. In Shakespeare's famous tragedy, *Macbeth*, the hero is told he will be safe until a forest comes to his castle, so he stops worrying ... until an enemy army attacks, after cutting large branches to hide behind! However, maybe Macbeth should have been worried from the beginning, because in fact forests have been moving about the Earth for millions of years ...

That sounds impossible, but in fact the logic is quite clear. Trees can only grow where the climate and environment will support them. But over long periods of time, both climate and environment can change. Perhaps the edge of a forest begins to expand as conditions become more favourable, or the place where the first trees grew becomes hostile and the forest retreats from it.

- How is forest migration the same as the migration of animals? How is it different?
- Over history, humans have also migrated. For what reasons?
- In some ways, forest migration is similar to human migration. What similarities can you think of?

LOOKING FORWARD >>

- What factors do we use to study population?
- Is the world population increasing or decreasing at the moment?
- Is the world population equally distributed over the continents?
- What are the consequences of the rural exodus?

1 Population growth

What factors do we use to study population?

1.1 Natural population change

A place's population can grow or shrink because of natural factors such as births and deaths. In order to study a population over time, human geographers therefore analyse birth and death rates.

THE BIRTH RATE

The **birth rate** is the number of **births** in a population in one year. It is measured by calculating the **crude birth rate** (CBR). The CBR tells us if the birth rate is high or low, and can be used to compare population change in different places. The CBR is the number of births per year in relation to the total population.

The crude birth rate is calculated using the following formula:

$$\text{CBR} = \frac{\text{number of live births in one year}}{\text{total population}} \times 1\,000$$

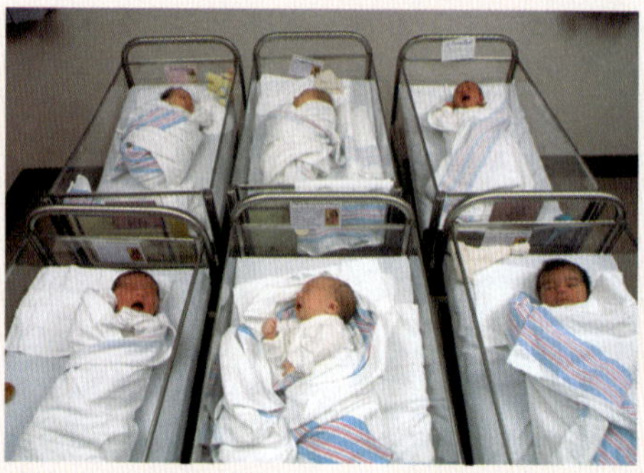

For example, in 2013, the German population was 80 767 463 inhabitants. 682 069 babies were born that year.

$$\frac{682\,069}{80\,767\,463} \times 1\,000 = 8.44‰$$

The birth rates in **developed countries** are less than 20‰. For example, Ireland has a birth rate of 15‰ and Germany has a birth rate of 8.5‰.

Less developed countries have higher birth rates, sometimes as high as 50‰. For example, Mali has a birth rate of 45‰ and Kenya has a birth rate of 26‰.

THE DEATH RATE

The **death rate** is the number of **deaths** in a population in one year.

It is measured by calculating the **crude death rate** (CDR) using the following formula:

$$\text{CDR} = \frac{\text{number of deaths in one year}}{\text{total population}} \times 1\,000$$

For example, 893 069 people died in Germany in 2013. The total population that year was 80 767 463.

$$\frac{893\,069}{80\,767\,463} \times 1\,000 = 11.6‰$$

The average death rates in **developed countries** are low.

Less developed countries have high death rates. The main reasons for this are related to poverty: hunger, bad sanitary conditions and war.

ACTIVITIES

1. What is the difference between the birth rate and the death rate?
2. What type of birth and death rate do developing countries have?
3. Search for information about the Spanish population. Calculate the birth rate and the death rate.

NATURAL INCREASE

By calculating the **difference** between the **birth rate** and **death rate**, we can calculate the population's **rate of natural increase**. If there are more births than deaths, the population **grows**. This is **positive** natural increase. If there are more deaths than births, the number of inhabitants **decreases**. This is **negative** natural increase.

The **rate of natural increase** (RNI) is calculated using the following formula:

$$\text{RNI} = \frac{\text{number of births} - \text{number of deaths}}{\text{total population}} \times 100$$

1.2 Other indicators related to birth and death rates

LIFE EXPECTANCY

Life expectancy is the average number of years a person is expected to live at the time of their birth. Women generally have a higher life expectancy than men. Life expectancy is linked to development: it is less than 50 years in poor countries, and about 80 years in developed countries.

Spaniards have the longest life expectancy in Europe.

GENERAL FERTILITY RATE

The **general fertility rate** (GFR) is the number of births in a place in relation to the number of women who live there and their age. When calculating this rate, women between 15 and 49 years of age are considered to be of childbearing age.

$$\text{GFR} = \frac{\text{number of live births in one year}}{\text{number of women aged 15 to 49 years}} \times 1\,000$$

INFANT MORTALITY RATE

The **infant mortality rate** (IMR) is the number of children who die before they are 12 months old in relation to the total number of births in one year.

$$\text{IMR} = \frac{\text{total deaths of babies under 12 months in one year}}{\text{total births in one year}} \times 1\,000$$

Babies under one year of age are more likely to die as a result of **malnutrition** or a lack of medical care. Poor countries therefore have a high infant mortality rate.

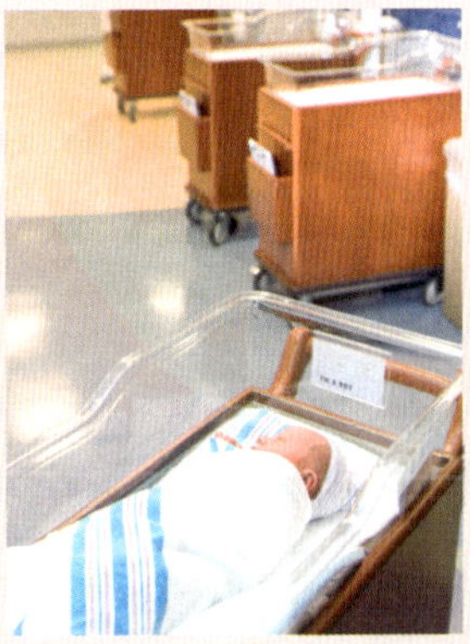

The infant mortality rate in developed countries is low.

BIG THINKER

Louis Pasteur's work was a milestone in preventing infections and reducing the number of deaths. As a student, Louis loved art and singing, but after his first science class he knew what he really wanted to be. When three of his children died from **typhoid fever**, he stopped teaching science and devoted himself to finding a cure for infectious diseases instead. He helped produce the first vaccines for rabies, but he is most famous for pasteurisation, the process that destroys dangerous microbes in our food and drink. What is rabies? What causes rabies?

ACTIVITIES

4. What is life expectancy? What type of countries have the highest life expectancy?
5. Is every woman taken into account to calculate the general fertility rate? Why?
6. What factors affect the infant mortality rate? Is the infant mortality rate the same around the world?

1.3 Migration

Migration is the **movement** of people from one place in the world to another. When people leave a place, it is called **emigration**. When they arrive in a place, it is called **immigration**. This means that the same person can be an emigrant and an immigrant depending on your point of view. For example, a Spanish person who goes to work in Germany is an emigrant in Spain and an immigrant in Germany.

1.4 Causes of migration

ECONOMIC

Emigrants move to wealthier places because there are more **job opportunities**.

Many immigrants in countries such as the United Arab Emirates have migrated because of better job opportunities.

SOCIAL

Social factors include opportunities for **education**, **healthcare** and **leisure** in the destination countries.

Many retired people migrate to countries like Spain because of their climate and tourist infrastructure.

POLITICAL

People emigrate to escape **wars** or political regimes in which they are **persecuted** for ideological, ethnic or religious reasons.

Conflicts such as the one in Syria force large numbers of people to seek **refuge** in other countries.

- Depending on its **causes**, migration can be forced or voluntary. Leaving a country for political reasons is usually considered to be **forced migration**. Leaving for economic or social reasons, on the other hand, is usually considered to be **voluntary**.
- Migration can also be classified according to its **duration**: permanent or temporary. **Permanent** migration means that immigrants do not return to their place of origin. **Temporary** migration means that immigrants stay in their destination for a period of time (this can be a long period, a season or even a day).
- Migration can also be classified into two types according to whether or not **borders are crossed**. If it involves a change in country, it is called **external** migration. However, if migration occurs within a country's borders, it is called **internal** migration. The most important type of internal migration is between rural areas and cities. This is called the **rural exodus**.

COMMUTING

In rich countries, people 'migrate' daily from their homes in the suburbs to their workplaces.

ACTIVITIES

7. Define 'emigration' and 'immigration'.
8. What reasons explain economic, social and political migrations? Give examples.
9. What does 'permanent migration' and 'rural exodus' mean?

1.5 Economic migration and its consequences

The **countries of origin** lose many of their youngest and most **entrepreneurial** inhabitants as a result of mass emigration. However, emigrants also send money back to their families, helping to **boost** the economy.

In the **destination countries**, immigration increases the size of the population of childbearing age, so birth rates increase. The arrival of young people of working age also contributes to economic growth.

There can also be difficulties with integration. These can be due to cultural, religious or language differences. As a result of these, immigrants may have problems integrating with the population in the destination country and may become isolated.

Economic migration in the world today

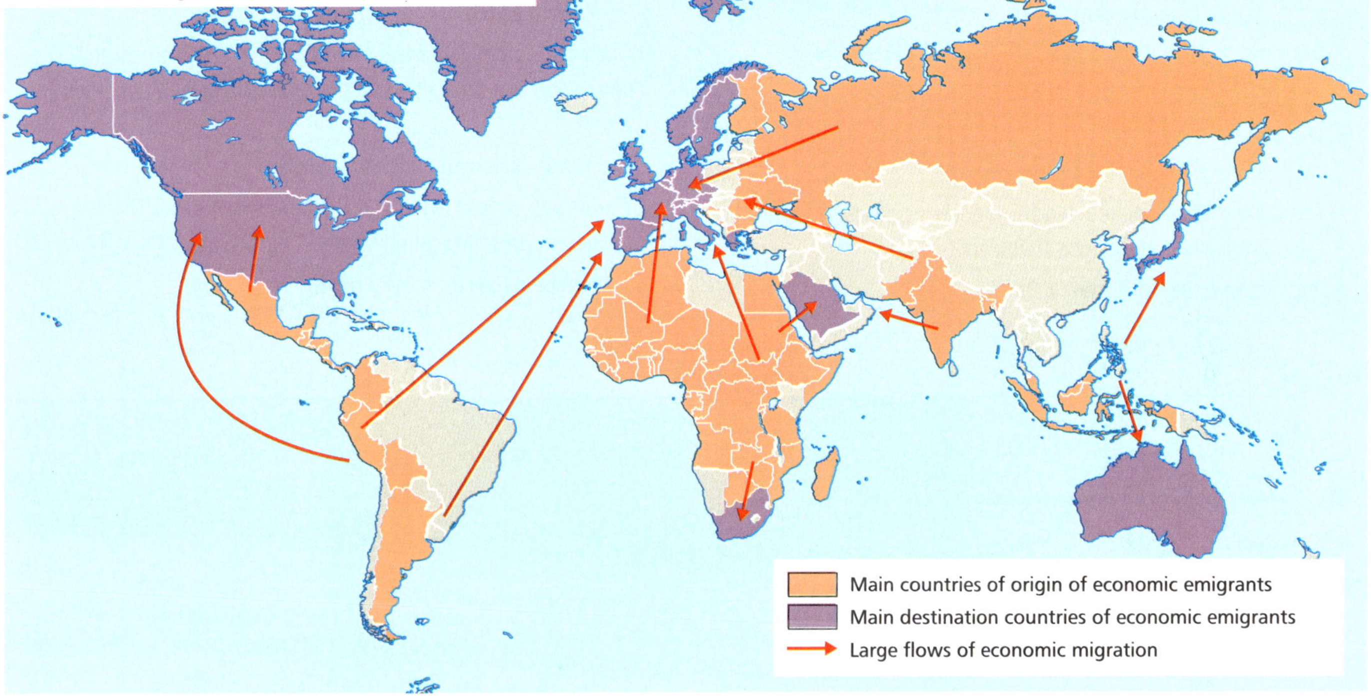

1.6 Actual population growth

We now know that variations in a place's population depend on its rates of natural increase and migration. To calculate the **actual population growth**, we therefore need to add the natural increase to the net migration. The result can be **positive** (if the population grows) or **negative** (if the population shrinks).

- **Natural increase**, i.e., the difference between the number of births and the number of deaths in a population in one year.
- **Net migration**, i.e., the difference between the number of immigrants and the number of emigrants in a population in one year.

actual population growth = (number of births – number of deaths) + (number of immigrants – number of emigrants)

CALCULATING ACTUAL POPULATION GROWTH

According to data from the Institute of Statistics of the Comunidad de Madrid, in 2013 there were 65 343 births, 42 393 deaths, 322 162 emigrants and 301 000 immigrants. Calculate the actual population growth.

ACTIVITIES

10. What are the advantages and disadvantages of immigration in destination countries? What difficulties can immigrants face?

11. Look at the map above. List five destination countries of economic emigrants. Explain why these countries are so popular among emigrants.

2 Population studies

Is the world population increasing or decreasing at the moment?

2.1 Demographic regimes

Throughout history, the global population's **rate of natural increase** has **varied**. The variations are reflected in **demographic regimes**: the combined birth and death rates over time. These regimes have been used to establish various **demographic models**.

1. OLD DEMOGRAPHIC REGIME

- Occurred in developed countries until the 18th century.
- The **birth rate** is **high**.
- The **death rate** is **high** because of poor nutrition, hygiene and sanitation.
- There are disaster-related deaths: sudden increases in the death rate because of war, hunger or epidemics.
- Population **growth** is **low**.

2. DEMOGRAPHIC TRANSITION

- Occurred in the 19th century and part of the 20th century in developed countries. It is still the regime in poorer countries today.
- The **birth rate** continues to be **high**.
- The **death rate** is **low** because of better **overall** living conditions and medical advances in particular.
- Population **growth** is **very high**.

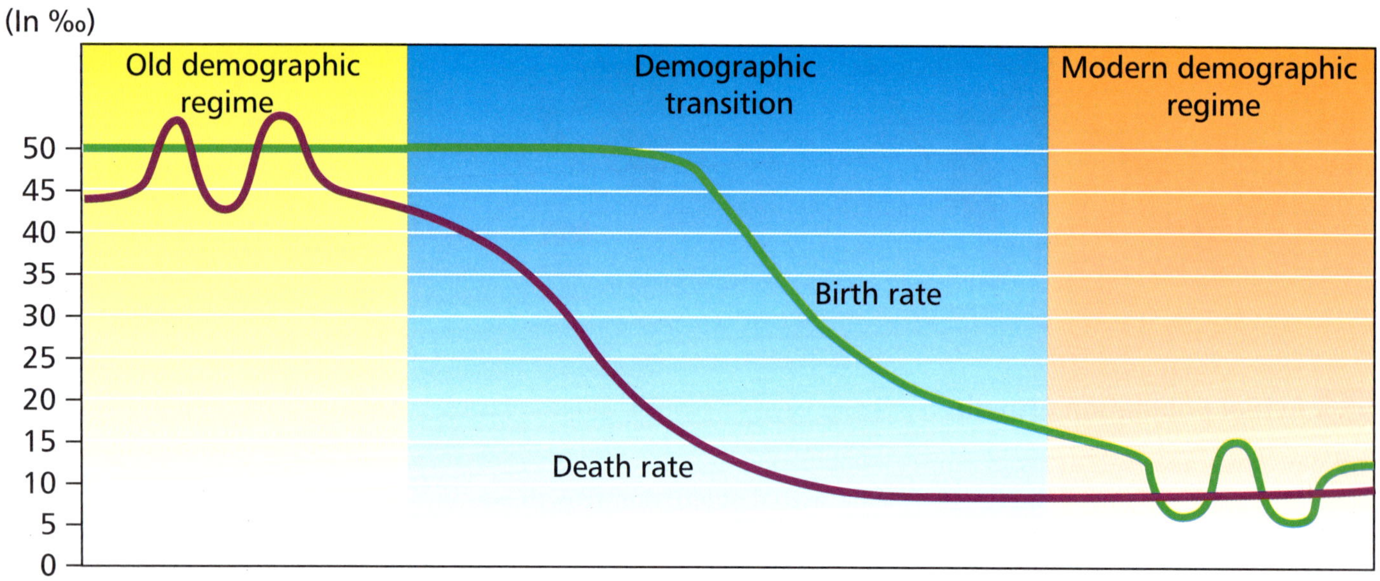

3. MODERN DEMOGRAPHIC REGIME

- This regime has developed in developed countries since the second half of the 20th century.
- The **birth rate** suddenly **decreases** because of sociological and cultural changes: more women in employment, new family models, development of **contraceptives** and family planning.
- The **death rate** is **low**.
- Population **growth** is **low** or **very low**.

4. REGRESSIVE DEMOGRAPHIC REGIME

- This model has been developing in some developed countries and may become widespread in the future.
- The **birth rate** is **low** with occasional **spikes**.
- The **death rate increases slightly** due to the ageing population.
- Population **growth** is **negative** because there are more deaths than births.

ACTIVITIES

12. What is a demographic regime? Why is it important to establish demographic regimes?

13. Which demographic regime will we have in the future? Why?

2.2 Population growth and decline

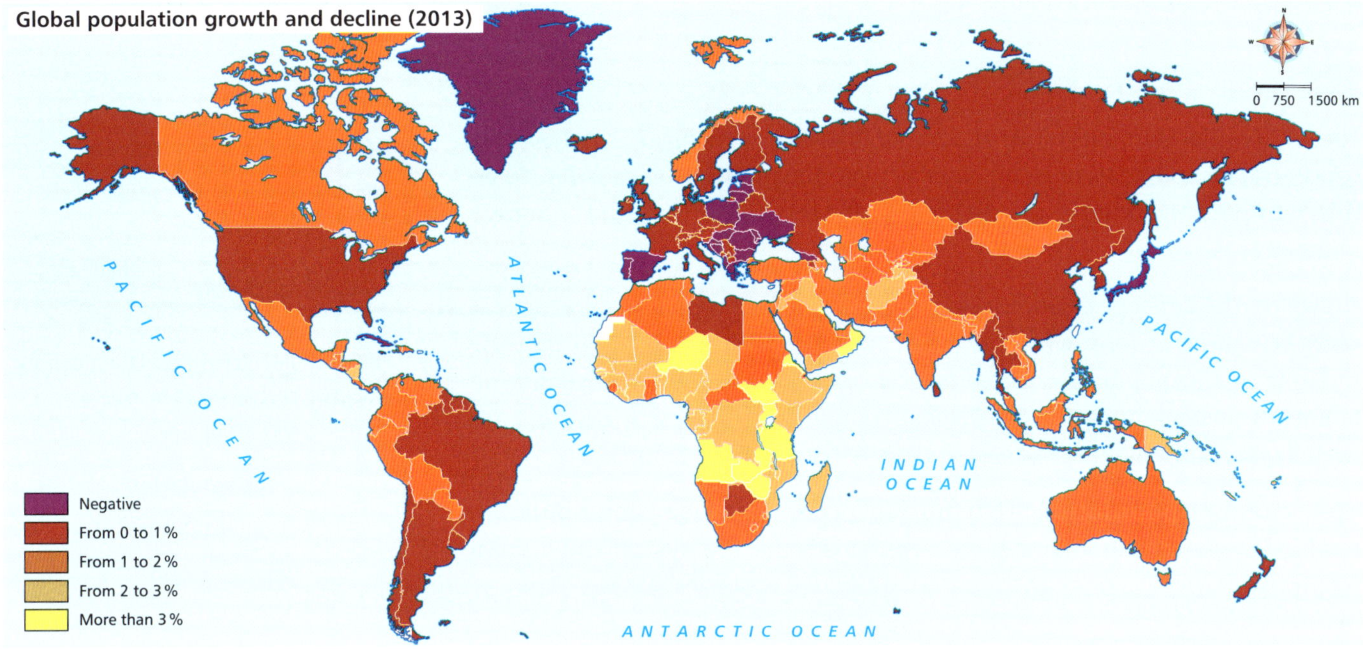

The **world population** is continuing to grow because the **rate of natural increase** is still **positive** in almost all countries.

The population growth rate has increased significantly in recent years. The world's population did not reach one billion inhabitants until the start of the 19th century. In just one century, the population doubled. Another century later, at the start of the 21st century, there were already more than six billion people. **Today**, the **world population** is more than **seven billion** people.

2.3 Population structure

Population structure is the composition of the population according to **sex** (male and female) and **age**. There are three age groups: children (0 to 14 years), adults (15 to 64 years) and the elderly (over 65).

POPULATION STRUCTURE BY SEX

The number of boys born is slightly higher than the number of girls. The numbers **even out** in adulthood because the male death rate is higher. In the elderly population, there are also more women than men because women have a higher life expectancy.

POPULATION STRUCTURE BY AGE

The total global elderly population is very small, just 8%. However, in developed countries, the life expectancy is high and the birth rate is low.

This means that these countries have large numbers of elderly inhabitants and the young population is small. The opposite happens in poor countries.

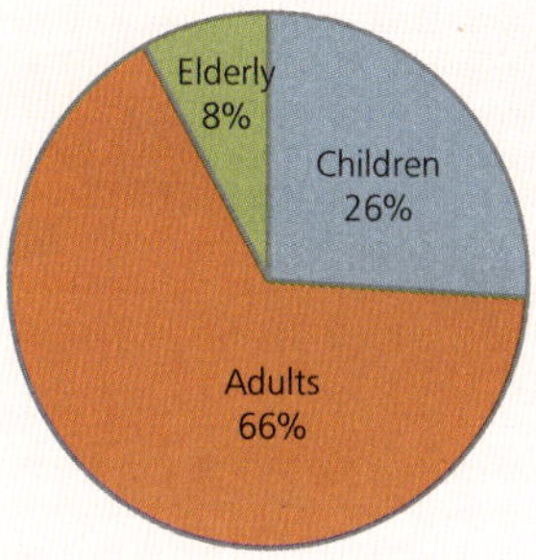

ACTIVITIES

14. Look at the map. List five countries for each of the categories mentioned in the legend.

15. What are the characteristics of the population structure by age in developing countries?

3 Humans in the world

Is the world population equally distributed over the continents?

3.1 Population distribution

The 7.523 billion humans on Earth are not distributed evenly. To analyse how concentrated a population is, we can calculate the **population density**. To do this, we divide the number of **inhabitants of a territory** by its **area** in square kilometres (km^2).

However, the concept of population density can be misleading, because it gives one number for a whole territory. This gives the impression that the territory and its population are completely uniform. Population distribution is not uniform: some areas are almost completely empty while others are very densely populated. This is particularly true in large countries.

This **unequal population distribution** occurs because the population tends to be concentrated in certain areas. This is due to physical and human factors.

POPULATION DENSITY

Population density is calculated using the following formula:

$$\text{Population density} = \frac{\text{inhabitants}}{\text{area}}$$

For example, global population density would be calculated as follows:

$$\frac{7.523 \text{ billion inhabitants}}{136\,100\,769 \text{ km}^2} = 55.2 \text{ inhabitants/km}^2$$

PHYSICAL FACTORS

The physical factors are related to the **geographical characteristics** of the place where the population settles. These factors affect how **resources** are used.

CLIMATE

Humans are more likely to settle in areas with **good temperature and moderate rainfall** such as **temperate zones**.

The conditions in cold and hot zones are not as good. Temperate zones usually have big populations.

RELIEF

People usually settle in **lowland areas** near the coast and river valleys.

The population density is low in **mountainous regions** because they are difficult to access, the terrain is steep and the climate conditions are not as good.

NATURAL RESOURCES

Humans need **water** to live. Populations therefore tend to be small in places where there is little water.

Throughout history, **soil** fertility has also been an important factor when humans have been choosing where to settle.

ACTIVITIES

16. What physical factors affect population distribution? Think of the place where you live. What physical factors does it have?
17. Population density can be misleading. Explain.
18. Search for information about the Spanish population. Calculate the population density.

HUMAN FACTORS

People can use technology to **modify physical factors** for their benefit. This means that areas where conditions for farming are not good can be successfully exploited thanks to water technology, seed selection, etc.

Economic conditions are also very important. People settle in areas where there are more resources, jobs and services.

There are also **political factors**. Governments can influence demographics by encouraging people to have children or penalising those who do, regulating migration or forcing citizens to leave for political reasons.

CITIES

The world population is concentrated in large cities. According to the United Nations, more than half of the world's population lives in cities. Mexico City, Shanghai, New Delhi and Tokyo are the most populated cities in the world.

3.2 Characteristics of population distribution

The distribution of the world population is characterised by the following:

- The Earth's **empty spaces** cover a larger area than the inhabited ones. Most of the world's population lives in just 20% of the planet's continental surface.
- The population tends to be concentrated in areas close to the sea.
- Most of the population lives in the **northern hemisphere**. The continents with the highest population densities are Europe and Asia.

Population density around the world

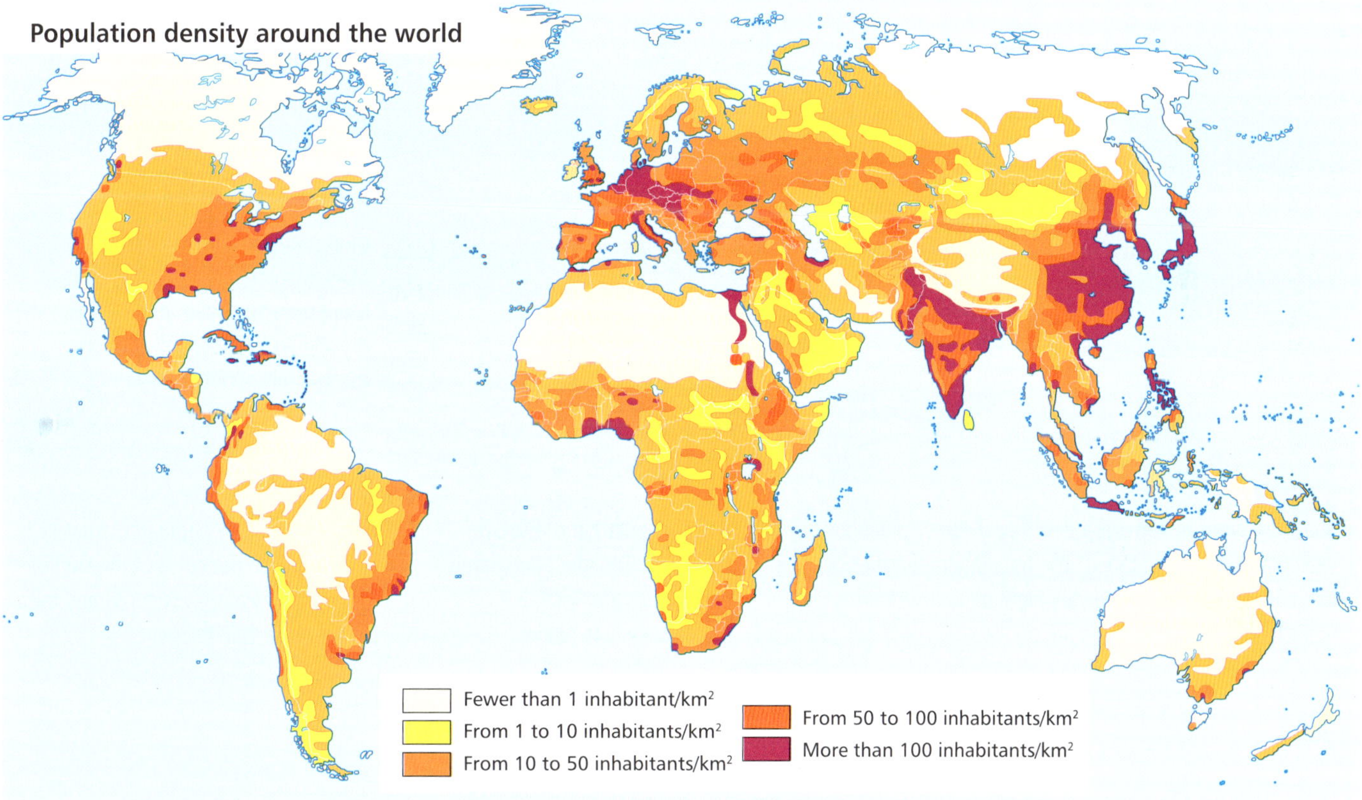

ACTIVITIES

19. What human factors are relevant in the population distribution?
20. What are the characteristics of population distributon around the world?
21. Look at the map above. Do India, Australia, Germany, Canada and Saudi Arabia show a uniform population distribution?

3.3 Highly populated areas

The most densely populated areas are in **Asia**. One quarter of the world's population lives in countries in East Asia, such as China, Japan and South Korea. These countries have a good climate for farming and people have lived in them for thousands of years. Other countries in South Asia, such as India, Bangladesh, Indonesia, Pakistan, the Philippines, Vietnam and Thailand, are amongst the most populated in the world.

DID YOU KNOW?

China has more than 1.35 billion inhabitants and is the most populated country in the world.

Populations around the world

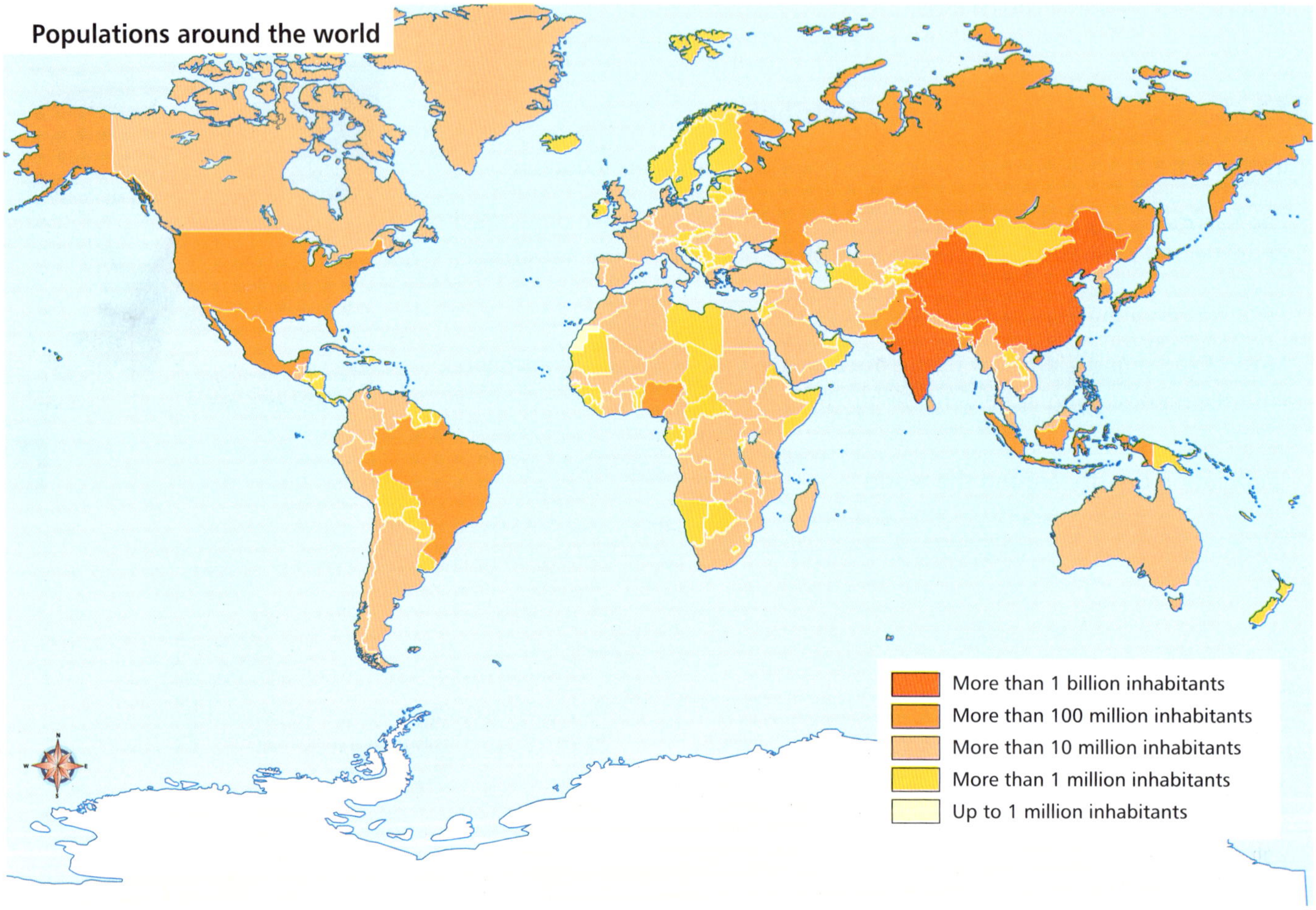

Some countries in **America** also have large populations (for example, the United States). The population densities of large cities on the east coast are very high. In South America, the highest population densities are on the coast of Brazil.

The population of **Europe** is large. The most populated countries are Russia, Germany and Turkey.

The most densely populated areas in **Africa** are on the coast of the Gulf of Guinea (for example, Nigeria) and the banks of the Nile in Egypt.

3.4 Areas with very low population densities

About 25% of the land on Earth is not inhabited, mainly because of physical factors.

Very few people live in **cold climate zones**. These areas are located in the polar circles or in very high mountain regions, and are usually covered in snow or ice.

In **deserts**, where there is almost no water, life cannot prosper. The Gobi Desert (Asia), the Sahara and Kalahari Deserts (Africa) and Antarctica are important examples.

In the **equatorial rainforests**, the vegetation is very dense and there is a lot of wildlife.

However, humans do not adapt well to the region's climate conditions.

3.5 The population in Europe

The population of Europe is very high. This is because of its **location** in the temperate zone, its **physical characteristics**, its **history** and its advanced **economic development**, with large industrial and tertiary sectors. These physical and human characteristics have led to the continent's current population of approximately **740 million inhabitants.**

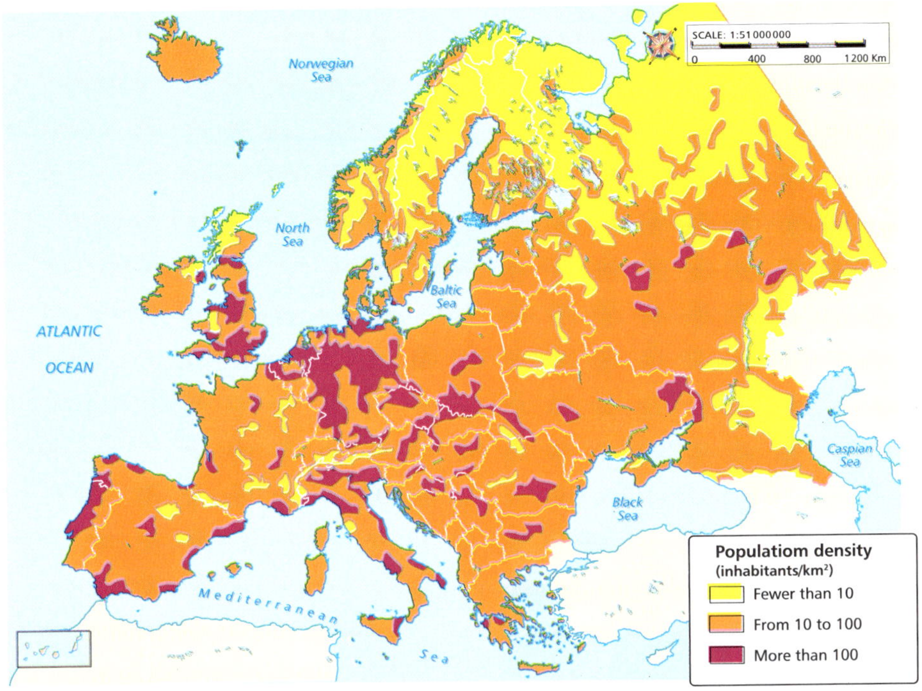

EUROPE'S POPULATION DENSITY

Europe's population density is about 70 inhabitants/km². However, this figure does not reflect the differences between different parts of the continent. In some countries, such as Belgium, the population density is more than 350 inhabitants/km². In others, such as Russia, the density is less than 10 inhabitants/km², even though Russia is the most populated country in Europe.

Moscow, the capital of Russia, is the second most populated city in Europe after Istanbul (Turkey).

Population growth in Europe has been very fast throughout history, especially since the end of the 18th century, thanks to industrial development. However, since the end of the 20th century, population growth has been very low. In some countries there has been no growth at all. **Birth rates are low**: the crude birth rate is between 9‰ and 11‰. In addition, life expectancy is high, so the **population is ageing**. Because of this, in the next few years the crude death rate is expected to rise. It is currently around 7‰.

Immigrants from other continents have also affected Europe's demographics. The arrival of young people from other countries has led to positive natural increase in countries such as Italy or Greece. Immigration has also affected the distribution of the population within Europe.

Today, countries such as Germany, France and the United Kingdom are popular destinations for immigrants from other European countries such as Spain.

ACTIVITIES

22. What reasons explain the Asian high populated areas?
23. Where can we find the most densely populated areas in America and Africa?
24. How does immigration from other continents affect the European population?
25. Look at the map above and answer the questions:
    a. What are the most densely populated countries?
    b. What are the least densely populated countries?
    c. What is the population density like in the north of Europe? Explain why.

4 The Spanish population

What are the consequences of the rural exodus?

4.1 Natural population change in Spain

Spain's demographic situation is similar to that of other **developed countries**. In other words, its birth and death rates are low, so the rate of **natural increase is low**.

SPAIN'S DEMOGRAPHIC INDICATORS

CRUDE BIRTH RATE	9.1‰
GENERAL FERTILITY RATE	38.82‰
CRUDE DEATH RATE	8.5‰
INFANT MORTALITY RATE	2.9‰
LIFE EXPECTANCY	83.0 years: 80.2 for men, 85.7 for women.

Source: INE (2014)

4.2 Migration in Spain

INTERNAL MIGRATION

Most internal migration in Spain has been for **economic reasons**. During the 20th century, people moved from the Meseta Central, Andalucía, Galicia, Aragón and Extremadura to large cities such as Barcelona, Bilbao and Madrid and to the Mediterranean coast, where the tourist sector was starting to develop. The main consequences of this **rural exodus** are high population densities in the major cities and depopulation of rural areas, where the population has aged significantly. The rural exodus slowed down towards the end of the 20th century, but its effects can still be seen in Spain's population distribution today.

EXTERNAL MIGRATION

External migration in Spain was very important **as of the end of the 19th century**. People emigrated for economic reasons.

At the start of the 20th century, emigrants travelled to **Latin America**. Later, between 1950 and 1970, they went to countries in **western Europe**, such as France, Germany and Switzerland.

From the **1990s** onwards, Spain became a destination country for **immigrants**, mainly from Latin America, Eastern Europe and North Africa.

This immigration helped lower the average age of the population, increased the birth rate and boosted the Spanish economy.

In **2010**, this immigration stopped because of the **financial crisis**. In recent years, Spain's **net migration** has become **negative** again. This is because many immigrants have returned to their countries of origin. In addition, some of Spain's young people are now emigrating to other European countries to look for work.

ACTIVITIES

26. What were the main destination cities during the Spanish rural exodus?

27. Where did Spaniards migrate at the beginning of the 20th century? Where did Spaniards migrate in the 1950s and 1960s?

28. Why did many immigrants return to their countries?

4.3 Actual population growth in Spain

Since 2012, Spain's **actual population growth** has been **negative**. This is because of the low rate of natural increase combined with negative net migration. In 2014, Spain had a population of about **46.5 million inhabitants**.

4.4 The structure of the Spanish population

There are **more women than men** in Spain: there are 104 women for every 100 men. Although more boys are born than girls, there are fewer elderly men than elderly women because women have a higher life expectancy.

The Spanish population is also **ageing**. When the elderly represent more than 12% of a total population, that population is considered to be ageing. In Spain, 18% of the total population is elderly. This population ageing is due to the gradual decrease in birth rates and increase in life expectancy.

However, Spain's population is not ageing equally throughout the country: Madrid and the southern half of the peninsula have a younger population, while the coast of Cantabria and inland areas have an older population.

4.5 Population distribution in Spain

Spain's **population density** is 92 inhabitants/km². However, the population is not evenly distributed.

The highest population densities are on the coast, on the islands and in large cities, such as Madrid and Barcelona. The population density is lower in inland and mountainous areas. The exceptions are capital cities such as Zaragoza and Valladolid.

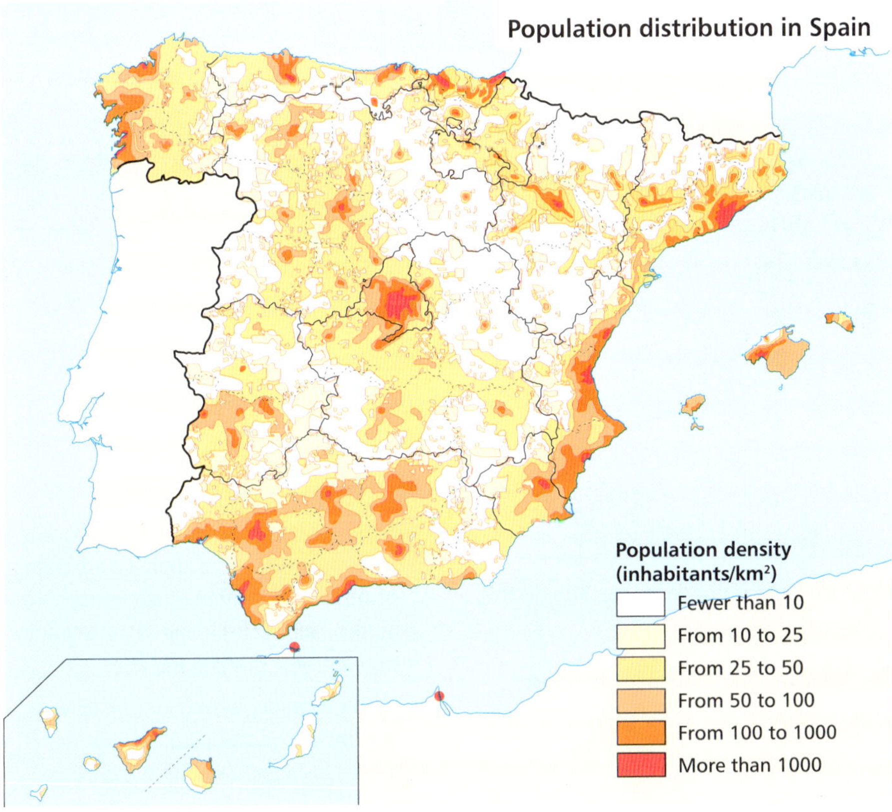

POPULATION OF SPAIN (2014)

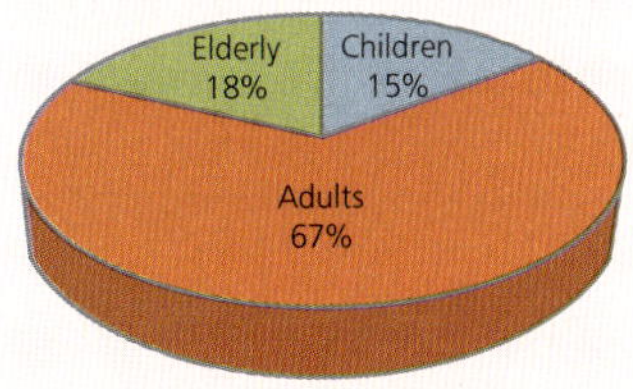

Population by age

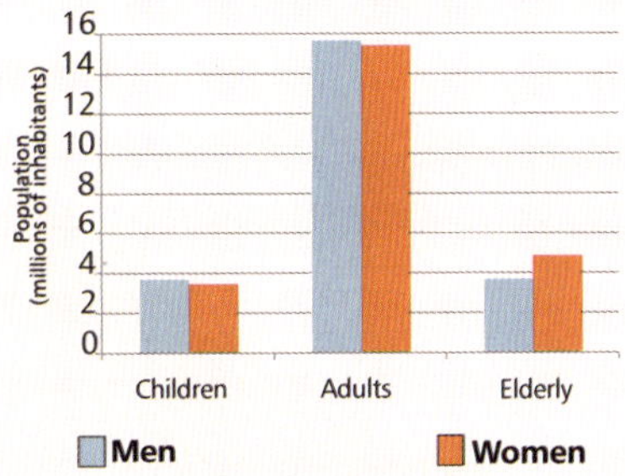

Population by sex

ACTIVITIES

29. Why is the actual population growth in Spain negative?

30. Which areas of Spain are the most densely populated? Why?

31. Why is the Spanish population ageing?

Discovery techniques

POPULATION PYRAMIDS

What is a population pyramid?

A **population pyramid** is a **graph** showing a **population's** structure at a given time. Population pyramids provide a useful overview of a population by **age** and **sex.** They can be used to analyse the current situation, the situation in the past, and the outlook for the future.

The pyramid consists of **two bar charts**. The two charts share a y-axis.

The diagram shows the **male population** on the left and the **female population** on the right.

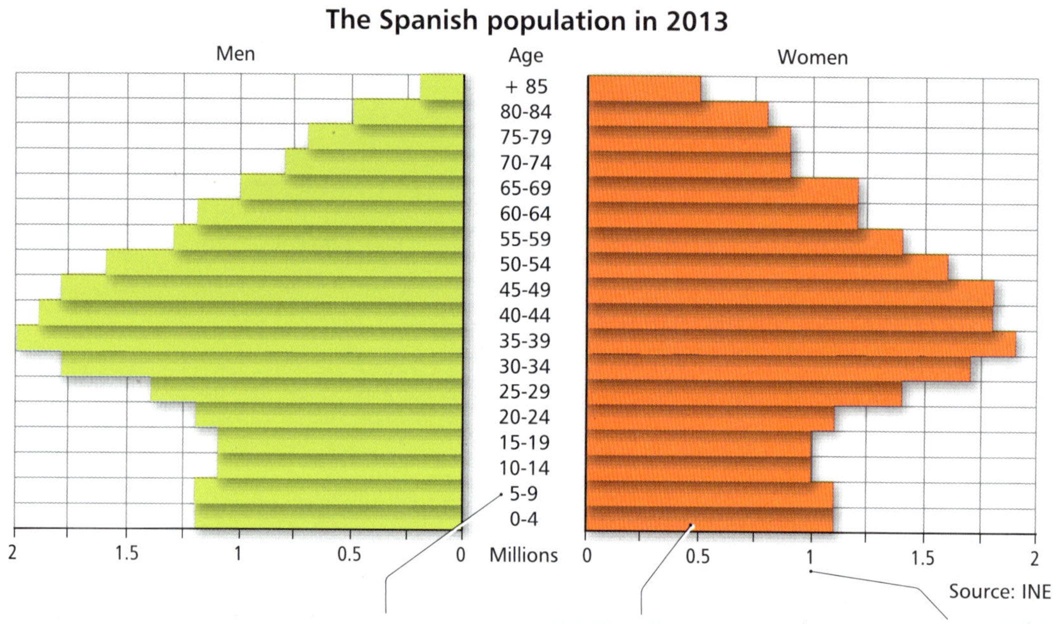

The pyramid **title** tells you the place analysed and the year the data were collected.

The **source** may also be provided. This is the name of the institution that provided the data used to make the pyramid.

The population is divided into five-year **age groups** shown on the **y-axis**.

The lowest age group (0 to 4 years) is at the bottom, and the highest at the top. The top bar includes all the people who are older than a particular age (in this case, 85).

The **x-axis** shows the population numbers. The numbers nearest the y-axis are lowest and they increase outwards.

The **length of the bars** represents the size of each age group. The size can be expressed as an absolute value (number of inhabitants) or as a relative value (percentage of the total population).

Analysing a population pyramid

To analyse a population pyramid, you need to look at the data it provides. You can do this by focusing on the following aspects:

1. Identify **population groups** by age. This analysis will tell you how many children, adults and elderly people there are in the population shown.

You can calculate the approximate **date of birth** of the different age groups. To do this, subtract the age of each group from the year given in the title.

In the example above, the first bar at the bottom of the pyramid represents people born between 2009 and 2013.

What type of information do population pyramids show?

The Spanish population in 2013

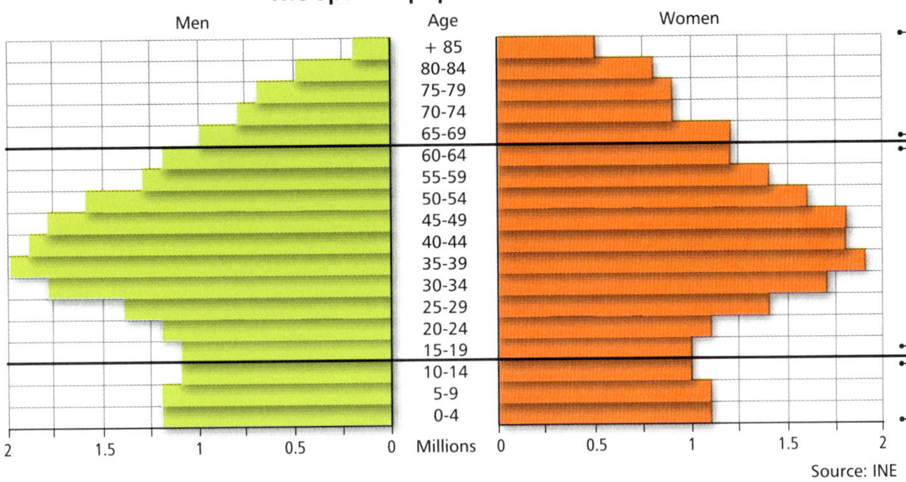

The elderly: 65 years of age and older.

Adults: between 15 and 64 years of age.

Children: between 0 and 14 years of age.

2. The **shape** of the pyramid. This gives you information about the demographic regime of the society shown. Below are some typical shapes.

TRIANGLE

A very young population with a high birth rate and low life expectancy.

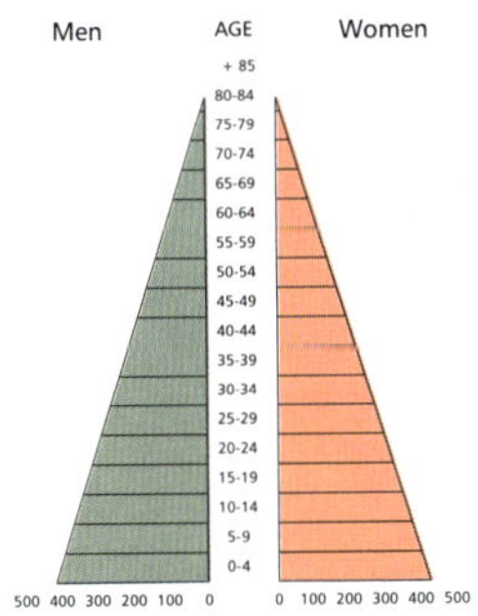

BELL

A population that has controlled death rates and maintains high growth.

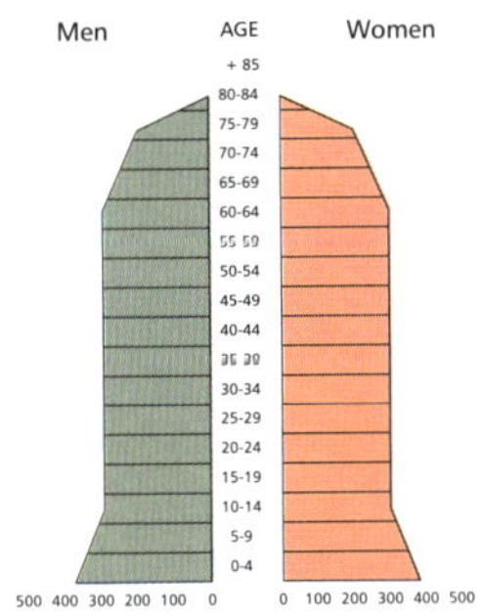

URN

An ageing population with a low birth rate and stagnating growth.

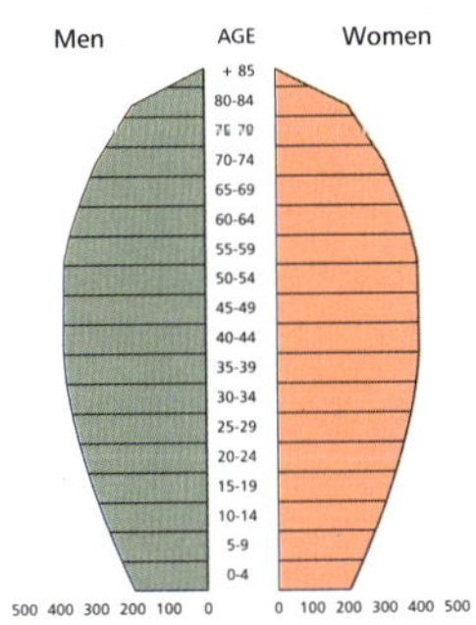

INVERTED TRIANGLE

A regressive, ageing population with a very low birth rate.

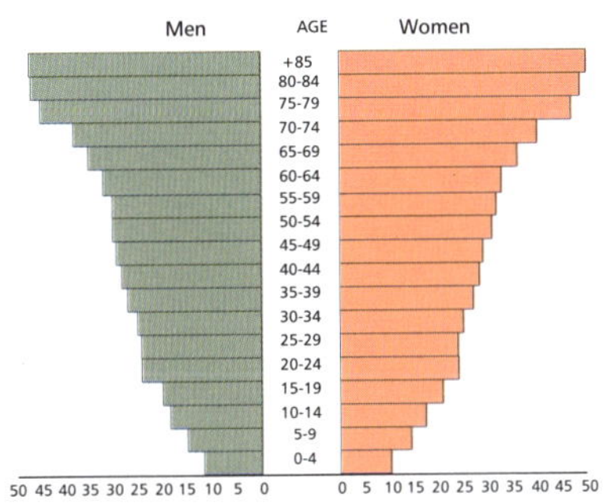

ACTIVITIES

1. Look at the population pyramid for Spain in 2013. In which years were the people in the largest age group born?
2. Look at the different age groups in the same pyramid. Are there more men or women in each group?
3. Look at the different pyramid shapes. Which demographic regime does each one represent? Describe the main characteristics of each one.
4. What shape is the Spanish population pyramid? Based on the pyramid, describe the population's main characteristics.

Revision activities

1 Look at the maps below. Analyse the fertility and infant mortality rates by continent and answer the questions.

a. Which countries have the highest rates?

b. How do you think these rates are linked to the level of development of these countries?

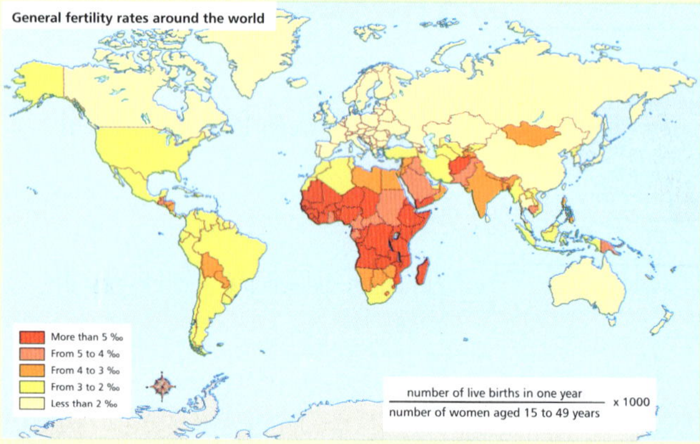

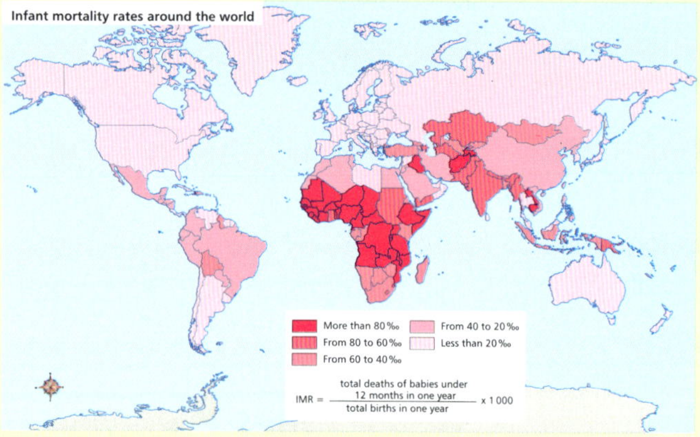

2 Look at the natural population increase map below and answer the questions.

a. Name 10 countries with high rates of natural increase and 10 with low rates.

b. Why do you think that the population grows more in some countries than in others? How do the birth and death rates influence this?

c. What role does natural increase play in migration? Why?

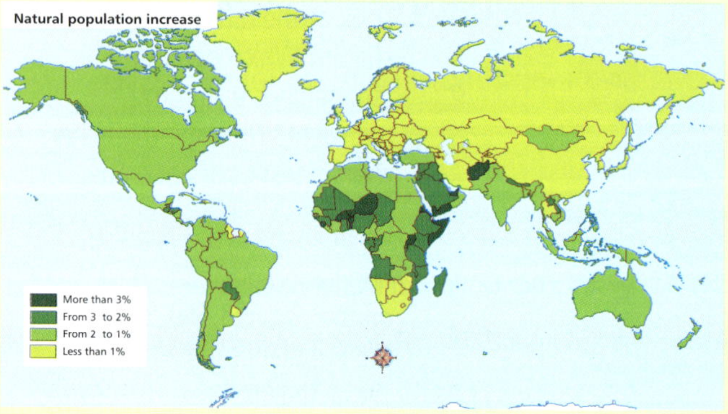

3 Use your calculator to complete the table of population density by continent below. Which continents have a population density higher than the global average? And a lower one?

CONTINENT	POPULATION IN 2014 (MILLIONS OF INHABITANTS)	AREA (THOUSANDS OF KM²)	POPULATION DENSITY
Africa	1 111	30 200	....
America	968	43 000	....
Asia	4 309	44 500	....
Europe	740	....	70
Oceania	....	9 000	4.22

4 What are the main characteristics of the population of Europe? Describe them in terms of the main demographic indicators and how they have changed in the last few centuries. What do you think will happen in the future?

5 Look at the map below. It shows the population densities of Spain's provinces. What characteristics help to explain the population distribution shown? Explain your answer.

6 Find the most recent population data for the Comunidad de Madrid on the National Institute of Statistics website (www.ine.es). Write down the total population, birth rate, fertility rate, death rate, infant mortality rate and rate of natural increase. Use the data you find to calculate the actual population growth rate in your town or neighbourhood. Which data will you need to do the calculation?

7 Look at the graph below. It shows population change in Spain. Answer the questions, then write a report describing your conclusions.

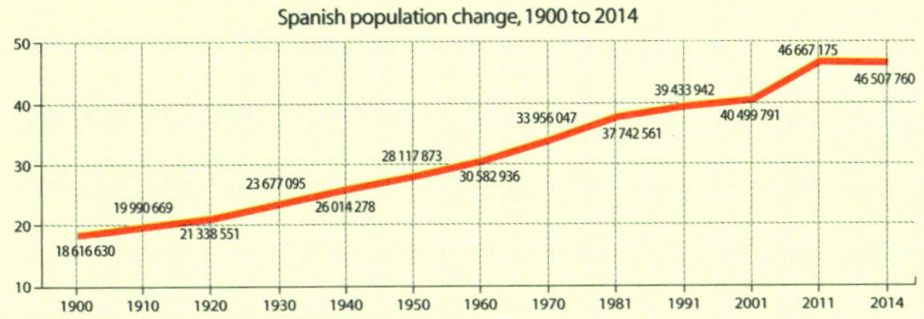

a. What was the Spanish population at the start of the 20th century? By which date did the population double?

b. During which decades of the 20th century was population growth fastest?

c. Analyse the data for the last 30 years. During which periods was the fastest growth? Describe the actual growth rate during the last few years. Explain how natural population change and migration have affected this.

8 Look at the two population pyramids for two Spanish regions below. Compare them. Write down the main differences between the population characteristics in each region and how they are related to the distribution of the Spanish population. Describe the causes and consequences of these differences.

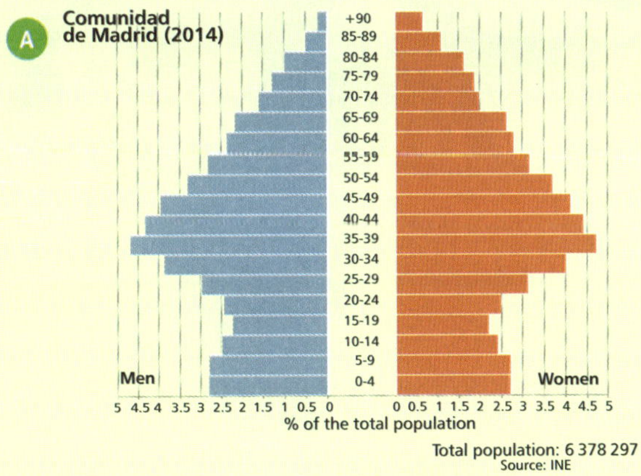

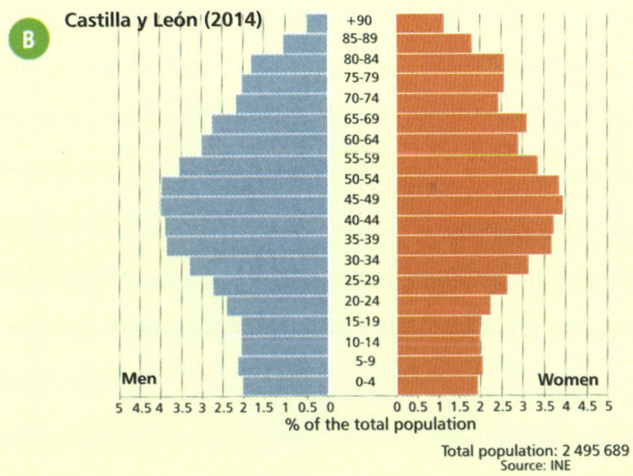

9 Search for the information about the world's most populated countries. List 10 of them and write the continents they are located on.

10 Read the text about Africa's rural exodus and answer the questions below.

> **"The fight to stem Africa's rural exodus**
>
> While Africa's cities are growing exponentially, Africans are leaving rural areas in their droves because they can no longer make a living from farming. A recent report by UN-Habitat found that 14 million people in sub-Saharan Africa migrate from rural to urban areas every year. Of those, 70% move into slums. This migration means more Africans will live in urban than rural areas by 2030, the report predicted. [...]
>
> According to recent research, rural exodus in Africa is compounded by the climate of sub-Saharan Africa, the development gap between the city and the rural areas, lack of basic rural amenities like water and electricity and lack of opportunities for young people. [...]
>
> Policies that can help reduce the risk of these kinds of natural disasters include introducing irrigation, insurance policies against crops failing, and drought-resistant crops. It is important to support farmers in preserving the environment. Rural communities have a critical role to play as custodians of the environment. We need to empower them to adapt their methods and mitigate the effects of climate change. [...]
>
> Nowadays, there are institutions showing that through a different way of working the land it's possible to live off the land and grow better food and have a better life. It is necessary to highlight the rediscovery of traditional techniques that have been neglected, such as composting and using animal waste as fertilizer."
>
> Source: Catriona Davies and Mark Tutton
> http://edition.cnn.com (adapted), December 2010

a. Why are people leaving African villages?

b. Why is it important to maintain people working the land?

c. What measures can be taken to help the rural areas?

Read and think

THE MOST DENSELY-POPULATED COUNTRIES IN EUROPE

The first country is a constitutional monarchy on the Mediterranean coast. It has an area of 2.02 square kilometres and its main source of income is tourism, although it has a small fishing industry. Tourists are attracted there because of its splendid scenery, its casino and its climate. Its official language is French, although other languages are spoken there. It has the world's lowest poverty rate and the highest number of millionaires and billionaires per capita in the world. With a population of about 37 800 people, the population structure is unusual as there are more French nationals than people born there. Apart from its casino, this tiny country is famous for a Formula One Grand Prix, which has been held there since 1929. Driver Nelson Piquet once said that driving round the circuit was like 'riding a bicycle around your living-room'!

The second country is an absolute elective monarchy and is inland. It is 1 kilometre long and 0.85 kilometres wide and one of its sources of income is tourism. The country obtains substantial revenue from museum entrance fees and from the sale of stamps, coins and souvenirs. Some tourists are attracted there because of its monuments but others go there for religious reasons. It does not have an official language but the language most commonly used is Italian. With a population of 842 people, the population structure is unusual as only 30% of the people with citizenship are women. This is because people acquire citizenship if they are given certain jobs there. When their jobs finish, they lose citizenship but are automatically given Italian nationality.

ANSWER THE QUESTIONS

1. What are the two countries described in the text?
2. What is the difference between the two countries in terms of government?
3. How are they different in geographical terms?
4. What attracts tourists to each of the countries?
5. What are the main languages spoken in each country?
6. Which country has the highest population density?
7. Why are both population structures unusual?
8. Why do you think that Nelson Piquet said that driving round the circuit was like driving a bicycle round your living room?
9. Why do you think that so few women have citizenship of the second country?
10. Who can be a citizen of the second country?
11. Investigate and discuss.
    a. Find out about one of the two least-densely populated countries in the world: Mongolia or Namibia. Note down the reasons for their low population density.
    b. Explain your findings to the class.
    c. What are the advantages and disadvantages of living in countries with very high or very low population densities?

Work it out

CONCEPT MAP

Use the words in the word cloud to create your own unit map in your notebook. Write any connecting texts you need.

by age climate social economic migrations
population distribution political population structure
elderly children **population** causes women
physical factors human factors
adults permanent or temporary relief
types men natural resources death rate internal or external
by sex forced or voluntary
birth rate natural population change

SELF-ASSESSMENT

Carry out a self-assessment of what you learnt in this unit. Choose one answer for each question and then check your answers.

1. Natural increase is the ...
   a. sum of births and deaths.
   b. difference between the birth and the death rate.
   c. number of births in a population.

2. Life expectancy around the world is ...
   a. the same in developed and developing countries.
   b. higher in developing countries.
   c. higher in developed countries.

3. Which population group is the largest in the world?
   a. children
   b. adults
   c. the elderly

4. The main causes of migrations are ...
   a. economic, political and social.
   b. economic, social and physical.
   c. political, social and historical.

5. In the modern demographic regime ...
   a. the birth and death rates are low.
   b. the birth rate is high and the death rate is low.
   c. the birth rate is low and the death rate is high.

6. To calculate actual population growth, it is necessary to take into account ...
   a. the natural increase and rural exodus.
   b. the birth rate and net migration.
   c. the natural increase and net migration.

7. Which areas show a low population density?
   a. coastal areas and deserts
   b. the poles and mountainous areas
   c. deserts and the poles

8. Currently, the European population has the following characteristics:
   a. a low birth rate and an ageing population.
   b. a high birth rate and an ageing population.
   c. a high birth rate and a young population.

9. Which Spanish areas received population during the rural exodus?
   a. Mediterranean coast and Extremadura
   b. Bilbao and Madrid
   c. Galicia, Bilbao and Barcelona

10. Spanish net migration is currently ...
    a. positive.
    b. neutral.
    c. negative.

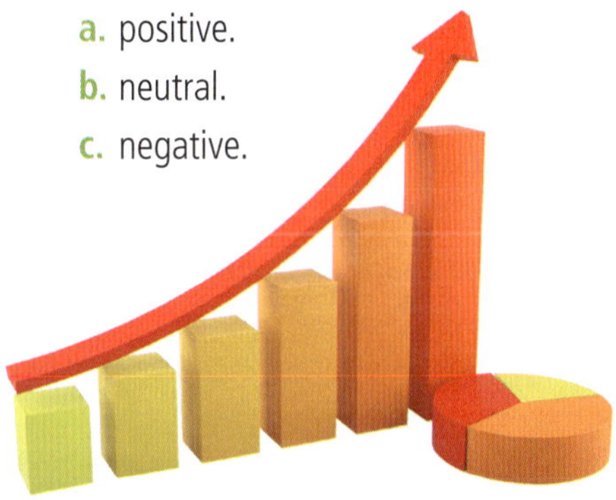

03 Urban areas

<< LOOKING BACK

- What is the difference between a village and a city?
- What are the advantages of living in a city? What are the advantages of living in a village?
- Look at photos A and B. What are some problems that cities face? How can they be solved?
- Look at photos C and D. Can you name the cities? What different functions do these cities have?
- What are the most populated cities in Europe? What are the most populated cities in Spain?

B

A

C

Ant cities

One day, the Wizard School visited an urban farm. Bobby saw some ants carrying leaves into a hole. 'Stupid ants!' he said.

'Ant nests are as impressive as human cities,' said his teacher, but Bobby ignored her. 'Time to teach him a real lesson', she thought.

The next moment – *pop!* – Bobby was smaller than an ant himself! He fell into the hole and landed in a pile of mouldy leaves at the bottom of the nest. 'How will I escape?' he wondered.

Then a *huge* ant started collecting the mould. Bobby jumped on the ant's back, and it ran down a maze of passages and chambers. He saw thousands of ants, some eating the mould, or caring for eggs and grubs, or expanding and defending the nest. He even saw the queen ant who was giving orders to the others.

'It's *just* like a city,' Bobby thought. 'I just hope this ant goes outside again before I have to eat mould, too!'

?

- What things does Bobby see in the nest that remind you of the human world? What might be the human equivalents?
- Most cities start small and get bigger (and all ant nests do!). What do you think are the first, essential things a community must have before it can grow into a city?
- What different places or activities does every city need to have? Which are the most important? Which need the most people to work?

D

LOOKING FORWARD >>

- What factors define a place as a city?
- What is the difference between developed countries and developing countries?
- Why was the 19th century important for the development of European cities?
- What are the two national metropolises in Spain?

1 The city

What factors define a place as a city?

1.1 The concept of a city

Urban areas have **evolved** throughout history. The process of concentrating the population in cities started about 7 000 years ago. However, the **fastest growth** of the urban population has taken place in **recent decades**. It is difficult to define the concept of a city, as **several criteria** are used to establish it.

POPULATION NUMBERS

It is easy to define a city according to this criterion, as cities have a **large number of inhabitants**.

However, the number of people needed to define a place as a city varies depending on the country. In Norway it is from 200, and in Japan, from 30 000.

ECONOMIC ACTIVITIES

Urban areas are dominated by activities related to **industry** and to **services** like health, education, banking, etc.

Meanwhile, in rural areas, economic activities are mostly related to the use of natural resources (agriculture, livestock farming, etc.).

STRUCTURE

Although there are some low buildings, cities are mainly made up of **tall buildings** that are very close together, and **public spaces** like avenues, squares and gardens.

However, in villages, the houses are low and there are fewer landscaped public spaces as people can enjoy the natural areas around them.

LIFESTYLE

In urban areas, personal relationships are less intense, **fostering anonymity**. Furthermore, people's attitudes mainly tend towards **speed** and **mobility**.

In rural areas, however, social behaviour is closer, more family-oriented and supportive, with a strong sense of belonging to a community and **attachment** to certain traditions.

ACTIVITIES

1. What economic activities are characteristic of cities? Give examples.
2. Why are there such differences between the definitions of a city as far as the number of its inhabitants is concerned? Consider the example of Japan and Norway.
3. What is the difference between rural and urban lifestyles?

1.2 The functions of the city

When we talk about urban functions, we are referring to the **main activities** that take place there or that most of the population do.

ECONOMIC FUNCTION

This is the main activity in most cities. **Industrial** cities, like Bilbao, bring together manufacturing and a workforce. **Commercial** cities are centres of exchange for all types of products and services. Transport networks (land, air and sea) and the flow of money from banks and multinational companies **converge** in these cities.

Rotterdam (the Netherlands) has a commercial function, as it is one of the world's most important seaports.

POLITICAL AND ADMINISTRATIVE FUNCTION

These are cities where the **political and administrative bodies** are located: of a country, like Madrid; of an Autonomous Community, like Mérida (capital of Extremadura); or of a province, like Lugo.

Moscow is the political capital of Russia and is home to its government buildings, like the Kremlin.

TOURISM AND LEISURE FUNCTION

Athens, Paris and Venice are cities with a **rich artistic heritage**, which makes them a tourist destination. Other cities like Benidorm, Monte Carlo and Las Vegas have **natural attractions**, like beaches and leisure infrastructures.

Venice (Italy) is a city that lives mainly from tourists who come to see its extraordinary artistic heritage.

CULTURAL AND RELIGIOUS FUNCTION

The existence of important **centres of culture and education**, like the universities of Oxford, Bologna and Salamanca, determine whether a city **fulfils** a cultural function. **Religious centres** also receive large groups of people on pilgrimages, as is the case with Santiago de Compostela, Jerusalem and Mecca.

The city of Jerusalem (Israel) is a centre of pilgrimage for Jews, Christians and Muslims.

ACTIVITIES

4. What criteria can we apply to distinguish an urban area from a rural area? What functions are there in urban areas? Use your ideas to write a report explaining the differences between urban and rural areas in Europe.
5. Cities usually fulfil more than one function. Explain why and give five examples.
6. What functions does Madrid fulfil?

1.3 How are urban areas occupied?

A city is divided into the outskirts and the city centre. The **outskirts** are the **outer area** which is bordered by the peri-urban area. The **city centre** is where the most important economic and social activities take place. It usually coincides with the old town, which is the oldest part of the city.

ACCORDING TO ECONOMIC ACTIVITIES

An urban area has different areas depending on the main economic activities carried out there.

INDUSTRIAL AREAS

They are mainly located in industrial estates on the outskirts.

COMMERCIAL AREAS

There are many large stores on the outskirts, while specialist shops are located in the centre.

BUSINESS AREAS

They are usually central areas with many tall office buildings.

ACCORDING TO RESIDENTIAL AREAS

There are two types of neighbourhoods in residential areas, which make up the largest part of the urban area.

WORKING-CLASS NEIGHBOURHOODS

They are located in the city centre or on the outskirts. They do not have many services or green spaces.

MIDDLE-CLASS AND UPPER-CLASS NEIGHBOURHOODS

They are located in developments on the outskirts or in the newer neighbourhoods in the centre.

DID YOU KNOW?

Islands aren't just in the ocean; urban heat islands are built-up metropolitan zones which are noticeably warmer than the areas around them. Energy trapped by modern building materials and released through transportation, industry, and other human activities can result in pollution and discomfort, and using air-conditioning can actually make things worse.

ACTIVITIES

7. What areas is a city divided into?
8. Give examples of economic activities that are carried out in the city centre and on the outskirts.
9. Where would you prefer to live: in the outskirts or in the city centre? Justify your answer.

1.4 Types of cities

Over recent decades, the **growth** of cities worldwide has intensified. This growth has prompted two phenomena which help us classify urban spaces: the **hierarchical system** of cities and the appearance of **new urban forms**.

URBAN HIERARCHY

Smaller cities **depend** on larger ones. In other words, they form an **urban network** with a hierarchical structure in which there are different types of cities:

World metropolises are highly-populated cities whose activities have **repercussions** worldwide because of their economic, cultural, technological or political influence. This is the case of New York and Tokyo.

National metropolises are the most important cities in each country. They are usually the capitals of the state or the most populated cities. This is the case of Brasilia and São Paulo in Brazil or Mumbai and New Delhi in India.

Communications networks and the main services of a geographical area converge in **regional metropolises**. Some examples are Casablanca in Morocco, Seoul in South Korea and Guayaquil in Ecuador.

Small cities are small or medium-sized cities that only have an influence on the towns around them. In Spain, this is the case of provincial capitals or county towns (for example, Toledo, Ciudad Real or Soria).

THE EMERGENCE OF NEW URBAN FORMS

METROPOLITAN AREA

This consists of a large city or metropolis and the towns around it. The towns depend on the metropolis for economic and cultural matters and jobs. Paris and London are examples of metropolitan areas.

CONURBATION

This is the **merging** of two or more cities as a result of their growth. Each city has its own administrative independence. Some examples are Rotterdam-Amsterdam and Liverpool-Manchester.

MEGALOPOLIS

This is made up of vast urban areas that extend beyond the regional level and are formed when different metropolitan areas and conurbations merge. Examples include Boston-Washington and Rio de Janeiro-São Paulo.

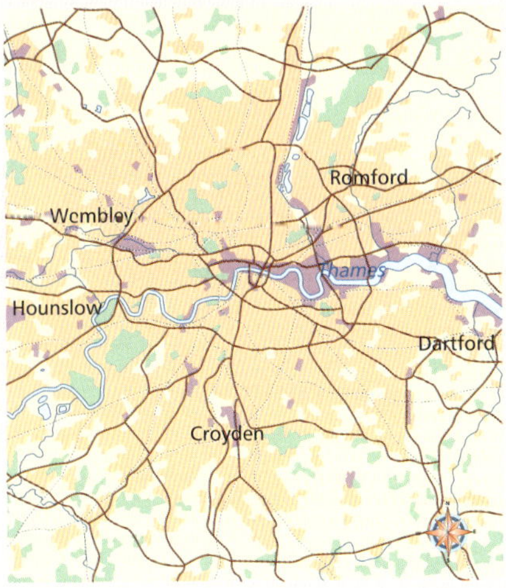

Metropolitan area of London

Rotterdam-Amsterdam conurbation

Washington-Boston megalopolis

ACTIVITIES

10. What function do world metropolises have?

11. List five Spanish cities. How are they classified in the urban hierarchy?

12. Give examples of economic activities that are carried out in the city centre and on the outskirts.

2 The urban era

2.1 The world's cities

Cities and their populations are experiencing **growth** on a vast scale. However, there are notable **differences** between the characteristics of cities in **developed countries** and those of developing countries.

CITIES IN DEVELOPED COUNTRIES

- In most of these countries, the increase in the urbanisation of land began in the **19th century**. The growing urban population led to the modification of city centres and **new neighbourhoods** were built near the old town.
- As of the **second half of the 20th century**, the centre was reserved for the construction of **modern buildings and** skyscrapers to form the city's **economic and financial area**. Meanwhile, the **residential area** was moved to the **outskirts** and the peri-urban area, where working-class neighbourhoods and neighbourhoods for the economic elite emerged. **Industrial estates** and, later, **shopping centres** were also built on the outskirts.
- **Today**, large cities are experiencing **slow growth**, which is compensated by the increase in medium-sized cities nearby.

Los Angeles

ACTIVITIES

13. Explain why industrial expansion in the 19th century changed urban areas.

14. Use the Internet to find out what cities looked like during the Industrial Revolution. What were the working conditions and living conditions like?

15. On which continent are the world's most populous cities? Explain the differences between them and say whether they are in developed countries or developing countries.

16. How do you think cities will change in the future?

What is the difference between developed countries and developing countries?

CITIES IN DEVELOPING COUNTRIES

The process of urbanisation in developing countries has accelerated over recent decades, as the rural exodus has intensified as a result of **population growth** and **industrial development**. However, there are **differences** in the **degree of urbanisation** of poor countries according to the continent. For example, urban development is high in Latin America, while it is lower in Asia and Africa.

Despite these differences, cities in developing countries share a number of **common features**:

- The tendency to concentrate the population in **large urban agglomerations**.
- Sharp **contrasts**, where luxurious neighbourhoods coexist alongside huge **shantytowns** that absorb most of the population.
- In general, they have a severe **shortage of housing and public services** like running water. In addition, there are many **social problems**, such as high unemployment.

Buenos Aires

17. Look at the maps and identify the cities located in developing countries.

18. Find out more about the cities in South America and Africa. How are they different from each other?

19. Think of the possible social conflicts that can occur in cities in developing countries. How can they be solved?

2.2 The advantages and disadvantages of urbanisation

THE ADVANTAGES OF CITIES

Cities offer a world of **opportunities** that **attract** a lot of people. This is because some **advantages of urban life** are concentrated in cities, such as:

- A more extensive and varied **labour market**.
- Better and more easily available **healthcare**.
- Numerous **educational and cultural activities**.
- Concentration of **commercial areas**.
- More leisure options.

THE CHALLENGES OF CITIES

However, the growth of cities is also the source of some **disadvantages** for the population, as well as **urban problems**.

SUPPLIES

Cities require enormous amounts of **drinking water** and **energy**.

URBAN WASTE

Large amounts of **waste** and **wastewater** are generated.

POLLUTION

Vehicles and factories give off **gases** which **pollute** the atmosphere.

HOUSING

The growth of the urban population increases the **demand for decent housing**, but the prices of houses or flats are very high in many cities. The most disadvantaged groups are therefore forced to live in slums.

TRANSPORT

Cities have **private and public transport networks** (metro, tram, bus, etc.). However, at certain times of the day, the infrastructure cannot cope with the quantity of vehicles. This causes **problems with traffic** and parking.

SOCIAL CONFLICT

A city is home to very different social groups and **problems with integration** can arise between them. They may be economic, such as the differences between rich and poor neighbourhoods, or religious and ethnic.

ACTIVITIES

20. Choose three problems that cities face. Think of possible solutions.

21. List the advantages and disadvantages of cities. Where would you prefer to live in the future: in a city or in the countryside?

22. Think of the challenges of cities and relate them to Spain. Do Spanish cities face these problems? Give examples.

23. Look at the list of the problems that cities face. Which two of them do you think are the most challenging? Why?

3 European cities

Why was the 19th century important for the development of European cities?

3.1 Distribution of European cities

The majority of the European population lives in cities, making it **one of the world's most urbanised continents.** The **development of industry** after the 19th century, following the Industrial Revolution, and the **abundance of services** have attracted people from rural areas. The **internal distribution** of European cities is the result of their **historical development**, which is reflected in their urban layout.

THE DEVELOPMENT OF EUROPEAN CITIES

- The continent of Europe has been populated for many centuries, so the oldest settlements are found within the city centre and make up the **old town**. The most important **monuments and historic buildings** are located in this area. Nowadays, they are often used for museums, hotels and offices of government agencies. Although these areas still retain their **residential function**, there are some problems, such as poor adaptation to urban traffic and the age of the buildings. This has led to the deterioration of the old towns in many cities.

In many cities, like London, modern buildings were built when the old town was restored.

- During the 19th century and the first half of the 20th century, cities grew because of the **increase in population** and the **Industrial Revolution**. This growth brought big **changes in European cities**. Therefore, additions and extensions were built next to the old town to house people. These streets were planned following a straight line, usually crossed by large diagonal roads to allow the movement of vehicles. There is **currently** a tendency to turn these areas into major **commercial areas**, **administrative centres** and company headquarters.

A major transformation of the urban area took place in Paris in the 19th century.

- The continued growth of the urban population during the second half of the 20th century led to the **transformation** of the city's **outskirts**. The main **industrial areas** moved there, close to the working class neighbourhoods. The wealthy classes also moved to the outskirts, so **residential areas** were built for the economic elite. In addition, communication networks linked to the centre of the city were built, making it possible to build shopping centres later. This expansion of the outskirts caused many cities to significantly **grow** in size. In some cases, they absorbed surrounding towns, so large urban conglomerations or even conurbations formed.

A conurbation of big cities, like Bonn, has developed in the Rhine-Ruhr region of Germany.

ACTIVITIES

24. Why did urban population grow in the 19th and 20th centuries?

25. What was the Industrial Revolution? Where did it begin? Why was it important? How did Europe change after the Industrial Revolution? What were its advantages and disadvantages?

26. Choose one of the cities listed below. Use the Internet to search for information about how your chosen city has developed over the centuries.

- Paris
- Moscow
- London
- Amsterdam
- Rome
- Dublin

3.2 Level of urbanisation in Europe

In **the United Kingdom**, **the Benelux countries** (Belgium, the Netherlands and Luxembourg) and **the west of Germany**, there are conurbations like Cologne (Germany), and Rotterdam-Amsterdam (the Netherlands).

Cologne

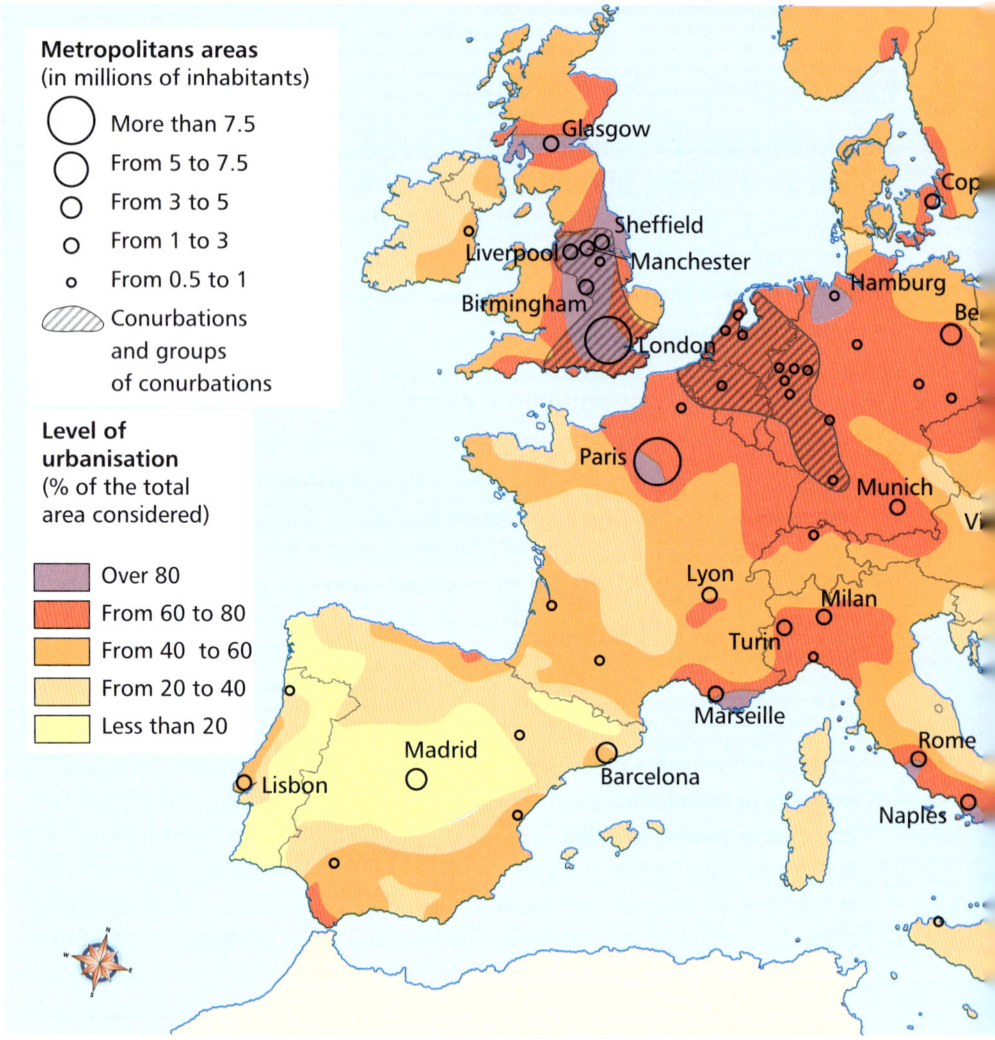

We can distinguish three **large metropolitan areas** or megacities: **Moscow, Istanbul and Paris**. In them, a big city has absorbed the towns and smaller cities around it.

Moscow

Istanbul

In the **Mediterranean countries**, there are medium-sized metropolitan areas, including capitals like **Athens**, **Madrid and Rome**, and important economic centres like **Barcelona and Marseille**.

Athens

Marseille

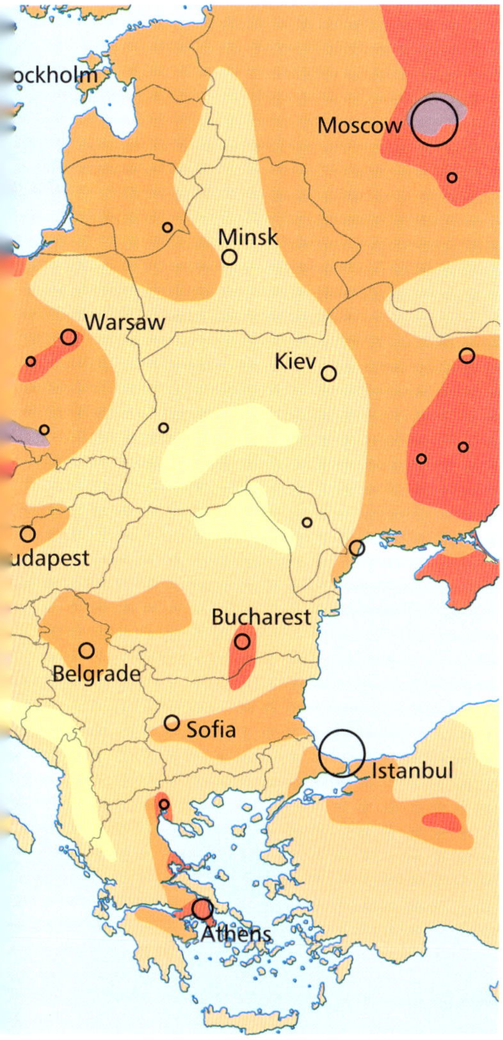

TYPES OF EUROPEAN CITIES

POPULATION

According to their **population**, large cities like Moscow or Istanbul are the most populated cities in Europe. They have over 10 million inhabitants.

However, there are also many cities with fewer inhabitants, such as the capitals of countries with smaller populations.

THE WORLD'S URBAN HIERARCHY

According to the **world's urban hierarchy**, there are two global metropolises (London and Paris), and other smaller national metropolises (for example, Rome and Lisbon), or metropolises on a regional level (for example, Hamburg and Munich). However, most European cities are small or medium-sized.

FUNCTION

According to their **main function**, there are commercial cities, like Rotterdam, financial centres, like Zurich, or places that attract tourists, like Prague or Venice. In addition, other cities have special functions, for example, religious, like Vatican City; there are also cities, like Brussels and Strasbourg, which are home to institutions of the European Union.

Zurich

Vatican City

However, the **main feature** of the European urban network is that **European cities** are **small or medium-sized**, especially when compared with the large urban networks in the United States and Japan.

Cartagena

ACTIVITIES

27. Look at the map. Give some examples of conurbations.

28. Geographically, where are the most urbanised regions of Europe located?

29. Look at the table which shows the main European cities. Then use a political world map to find which country each one is in and the capitals of these countries.

The biggest cities in Europe			
1. London	6. Amsterdam	11. Vienna	16. Prague
2. Paris	7. Frankfurt	12. Copenhagen	17. Lisbon
3. Berlin	8. Stockholm	13. Milan	18. Dublin
4. Madrid	9. Barcelona	14. Hamburg	19. Warsaw
5. Munich	10. Brussels	15. Lyon	20. Manchester

Source: Ranking of European cities (2013)

4 Spain, an urbanised country

What are the two national metropolises in Spain?

4.1 The urban phenomenon in Spain

Within the European context, Spain is a highly urbanised country with a model of **small** or **medium-sized cities**.

According to the National Statistics Institute (INE), in Spain a place is considered a city if it has **over 10 000** inhabitants and if its activities are mainly conducted in the secondary and tertiary sectors.

Places with between **2 000** and **10 000** inhabitants are towns, while places with a population smaller than this are villages.

Cities are distributed throughout the territory of Spain and certain **dependency relationships** are established between them, creating an **urban hierarchy**.

THE URBAN STRUCTURE IN SPAIN

National metropolises: Madrid and Barcelona. Their activities go beyond the Spanish borders, and cover all types of urban functions.

Barcelona

Regional metropolises: Sevilla, Málaga, Valencia and Zaragoza. Their activities extend throughout an autonomous community. Their main functions are administrative, commercial and industrial.

Sevilla

Sub-regional cities: There are 23 Spanish cities that control a specific area of an autonomous community. They specialise in certain industrial and service functions.

Granada

There are 36 **provincial cities** that control a province. Their activities are mainly administrative and commercial.

Toledo

Spain has two **Autonomous Cities**: Ceuta and Melilla.

Melilla

THE MOST POPULATED CITIES IN SPAIN

Cities	Number of inhabitants
Madrid	3 602 386
Barcelona	1 165 235
Valencia	786 424
Sevilla	696 676
Zaragoza	666 058
Málaga	566 913
Murcia	439 712
Palma de Mallorca	399 093
Las Palmas de Gran Canaria	382 283
Bilbao	342 574
Alicante	332 067
Córdoba	328 041
Valladolid	306 830

Source: INE (2014)

BIG THINKER

When he was young, **Frank Gehry's** grandmother encouraged him to make cities out of scraps of wood from his grandfather's hardware store. When he became an architect many years later, these experiences greatly influenced him. His buildings often feature unusual materials and sweeping shapes (like the Guggenheim Museum in Bilbao) and he is considered unique and experimental, rarely following a particular style. Many of his creations look like they are only half-finished, or made from recycled materials. Why do you think his artistic philosophy is important today?

ACTIVITIES

30. Look at the map on page 48. Identify the most populated cities. Classify them according to their urban hierarchy.

31. What functions do Madrid and Barcelona cover?

32. What is the difference between sub-regional and provincial cities?

33. Think of the place where you live. Is it a village, a town or a city? What functions does it fulfil?

34. What types of cities are the most common in Spain?

35. Why are Sevilla, Málaga, Valencia and Zaragoza considered regional metropolises?

4.2 The Spanish urban network

The Spanish urban network is not independent, but is integrated into the European network as an extension of its Mediterranean axis. **Urban areas** in Spain are related to each other in a **peripheral layout**, generated by the dynamism of coastal cities and island groups, with a **centralised layout** around the country's capital.

Madrid's political, economic and cultural importance means that urban flows and relationships are focused on this city. Spain has a peripheral layout, and except for Madrid and Zaragoza, the most important cities are located on the coasts, like Barcelona, Valencia, Sevilla and Málaga.

Madrid

Jerez de la Frontera

Pamplona

Palma de Mallorca

Vigo

Málaga

4.3 The development of Spanish cities

The Spanish urban network changed during the 19th century. From this time, Spanish cities experienced significant growth that led them to make changes in their urban layout, as had other European cities. These alterations and extensions are known as *ensanches* in Spanish. Notable cases are Madrid and Barcelona.

Barcelona

The increase in the urbanisation of Spanish society **began** in the **19th** and **20th centuries**. However, the **greatest** expansion took place in the 1960s, as a result of **industrial development** and **rural exodus**. This process was most intense in a dozen cities that dramatically increased their population and urbanised area.

An abandoned village

In addition, as the cities grew, so did the towns nearby. They became **satellite** cities or **dormitory towns**, where people live and then go to work in the big city during the day. This process led to major metropolitan areas, like Madrid, Barcelona, Valencia and Bilbao.

In **recent years**, the **growth** of cities has **slowed**, causing a gradual **loss of population**. The increasing cost of housing, relocation of industry and the improvement of transport means that many people have **moved to places** that are **further** from the metropolitan area. This is why **areas of continuous urbanisation** have emerged, like Corredor del Henares in Madrid and Vallès Oriental in Barcelona.

DID YOU KNOW?

Some cities with centuries of tradition are embracing a new future. Copenhagen, Amsterdam and other 'smart cities' are turning to new (and old) technologies like renewable energy sources (and bicycles!) to help combat environmental problems, and use cutting-edge information strategies to open the doors to 21st-century employment opportunities.

A bicycle parking station in Amsterdam

ACTIVITIES

36. Explain the process of the rural exodus. What were its causes? What were its consequences?

37. Look at the following aerial photograph of the city of Madrid and complete the labels that show the structure of the city. Use this information to write a short report on the development of Spanish cities.

Discovery techniques

AN URBAN PLAN

What is an urban plan?

A plan is a **graphic representation** of a **space drawn to scale**. In the case of an urban plan, the space represented is a city. Looking at the plan allows us to identify the morphology of a city when we recognise its form and structure, or in other words, the different ways the land is used.

The form of cities

The **morphology** of a city is the **spatial distribution** of urban elements: streets, buildings, green spaces, etc. These elements respond to a particular organisation or urban plan. There are four main types of **urban plans**.

TYPES OF URBAN PLANS

GRID

It is also known as a chequerboard or orthogonal plan. In this type of city plan, the streets intersect at right angles, forming a grid, and the space is divided into blocks.

Manhattan (New York, United States)

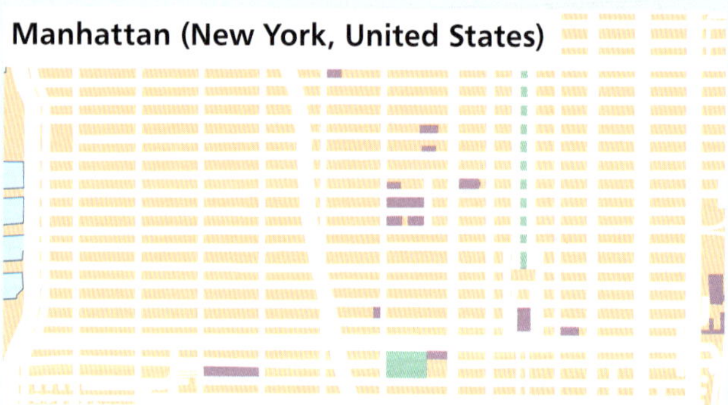

RADIAL

A central core can be clearly seen in a radial plan; this is the old town. Several roads branch from the centre like spokes on a wheel. In turn, they are intersected by streets that form concentric rings.

Moscow (Russia)

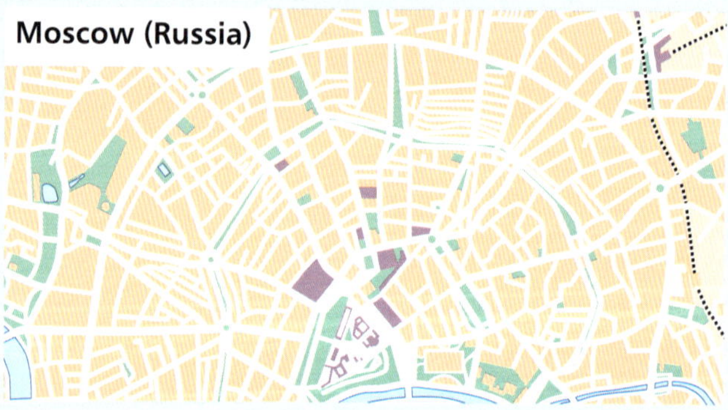

LINEAR

The city's buildings and public spaces are distributed around a main road. Their origin can be planned or respond to spontaneous growth around this road.

Logroño

IRREGULAR

This type of plan is caused by a lack of planning. It has a very complex and disorderly network of streets, roads of all sizes, squares with no definite shape and dead ends.

Toulouse (France)

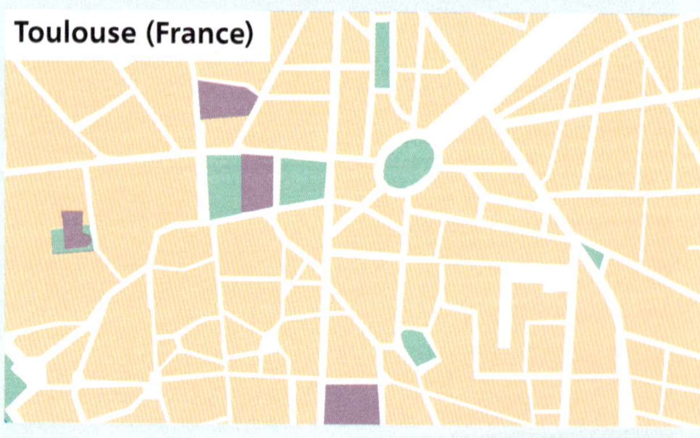

What do we use urban plans for?

Urban structure

A city plan allows us to identify the different **uses of urban land**. Once we have identified the **centre** and the **outskirts** of the city, the plan can help us locate different areas depending on their economic and residential uses.

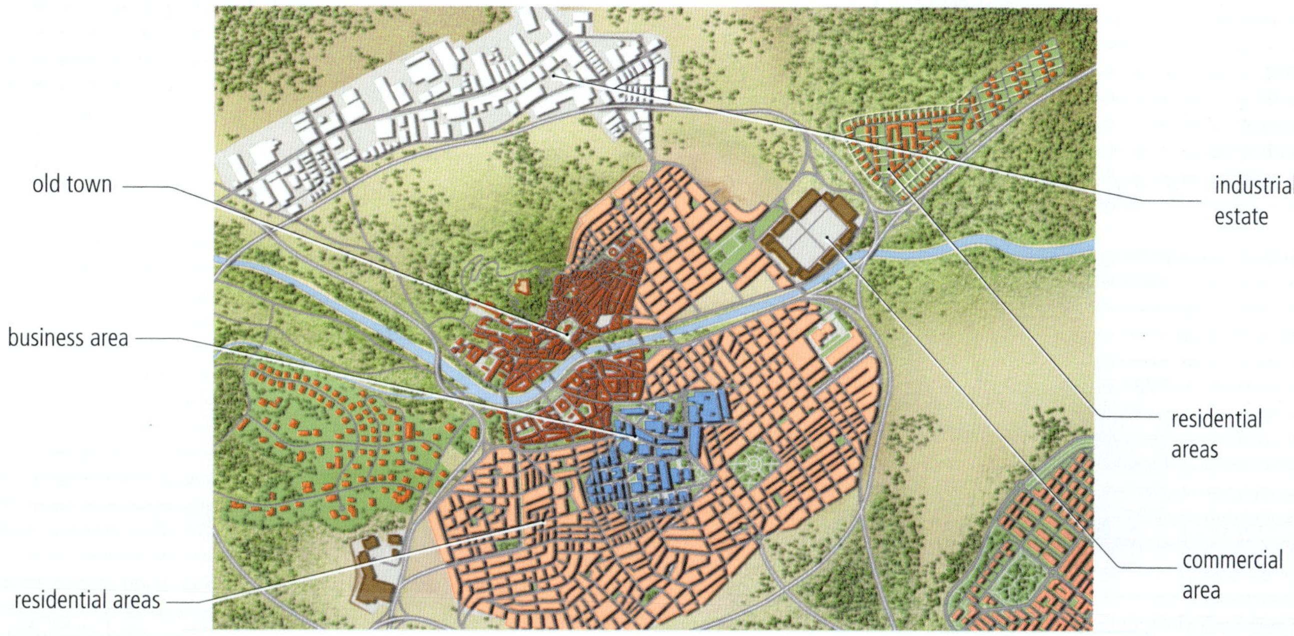

A plan can also show leisure and service infrastructures (like sports areas and schools, parks and green areas, etc.), as well as the road network: highways, roads, railway lines or pedestrian areas.

ACTIVITIES

1. Identify the type of urban plan shown in each photo. Give reasons for your answer.

A

B

2. Look at the following urban plan and describe what appears on it. Explain the difference between the centre and the outskirts and indicate how the land is used in each area. Also identify the main infrastructures, green areas and the road network.

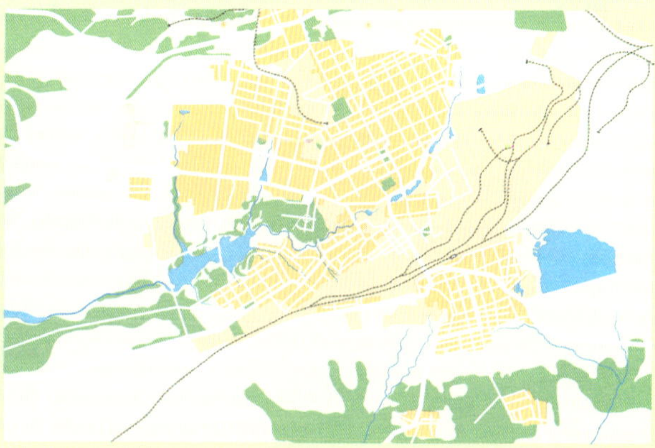

Revision activities

1 Look at these photos of different areas of Lisbon. Now say what point in the historical development of European cities you would associate with each one. Explain your answer.

A

B

C

2 Look at the two photos and explain the main differences between the cities in developed countries and in developing countries.

A

B

3 List the different functions of the city and give examples of Spanish cities for each one.

4 Read the following news article and answer the questions.

> **“Sixty-three percent of *madrileños* believe that pollution is the worst thing about the city.**
>
> Sixty-three percent of the residents of Madrid say that what bothers them most about their city is pollution, followed by noise, which is considered the worst aspect of the capital of Spain by 46% of its inhabitants. A study carried out by Ipsos in nine cities around the world (Madrid, Barcelona, Paris, Warsaw, Algiers, Rio de Janeiro, Chicago, Mumbai and Chongqing, in China) argues that Madrid is the city with the biggest problem with pollution after Chongqing.
>
> The report, called *Happiness in the City,* analyses inhabitants' satisfaction with different aspects of the city. In the case of Madrid, the other variables fall far short of these two environmental concerns. It is followed by insecurity and difficulty in finding work (19%), difficulty in travelling around (14%), difficulty in finding housing (11%) and unfriendliness (8%). Pollution and noise, as well as access to employment, are above the average of the nine cities.
>
> Only one in five residents in Madrid and one in four residents in Barcelona consider that housing prices allow them to own a home. The study argues that inhabitants of these Spanish cities, along with Algiers and Paris, are the ones who have the most problems when trying to buy a home.”
>
> C. Morales, *El País*, September 2014 (translated and adapted)

a. What percent of *madrileños* think that they can afford to buy a house?
b. Which cities have the biggest problems with housing?
c. What are the two biggest problems *madrileños* face?
d. Which city is considered to have the biggest problem with pollution?

5 Write a short text on the advantages and disadvantages of urbanisation. You should discuss the opportunities that are available in urban areas and the challenges faced by cities. Focus your discussion on European cities.

6 Look at these two photos and use them to explain the main differences between a typical American city and European one.

A

Chicago

B

Cracow

7 Divide into three groups and do a project on the types of cities in Europe. Each group will be assigned a criterion used to classify cities. Use it to indicate what types of cities there are in Europe and make a presentation with pictures to illustrate each one. You can display your presentation using a slideshow program or other IT tools, such as an interactive mural.

8 Look at the map below and do the following activities:

a. Identify the cities marked with a number. Use a political map to help you.

b. Look at the following graph on the world's most populous cities. Next, draw a table for each continent. In it, write the biggest urban agglomerations in order according to their population size, and say which number on the map they correspond to.

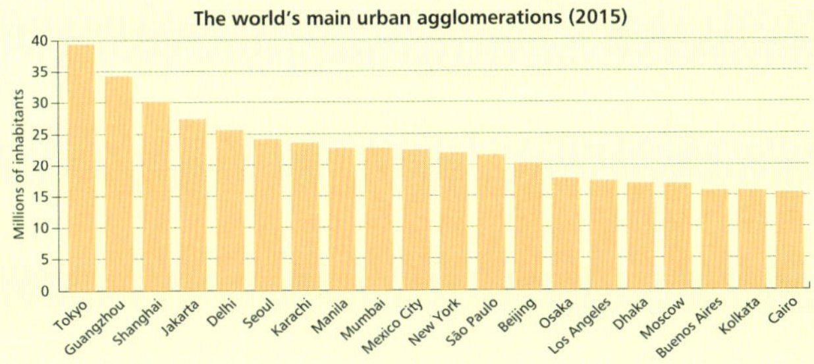

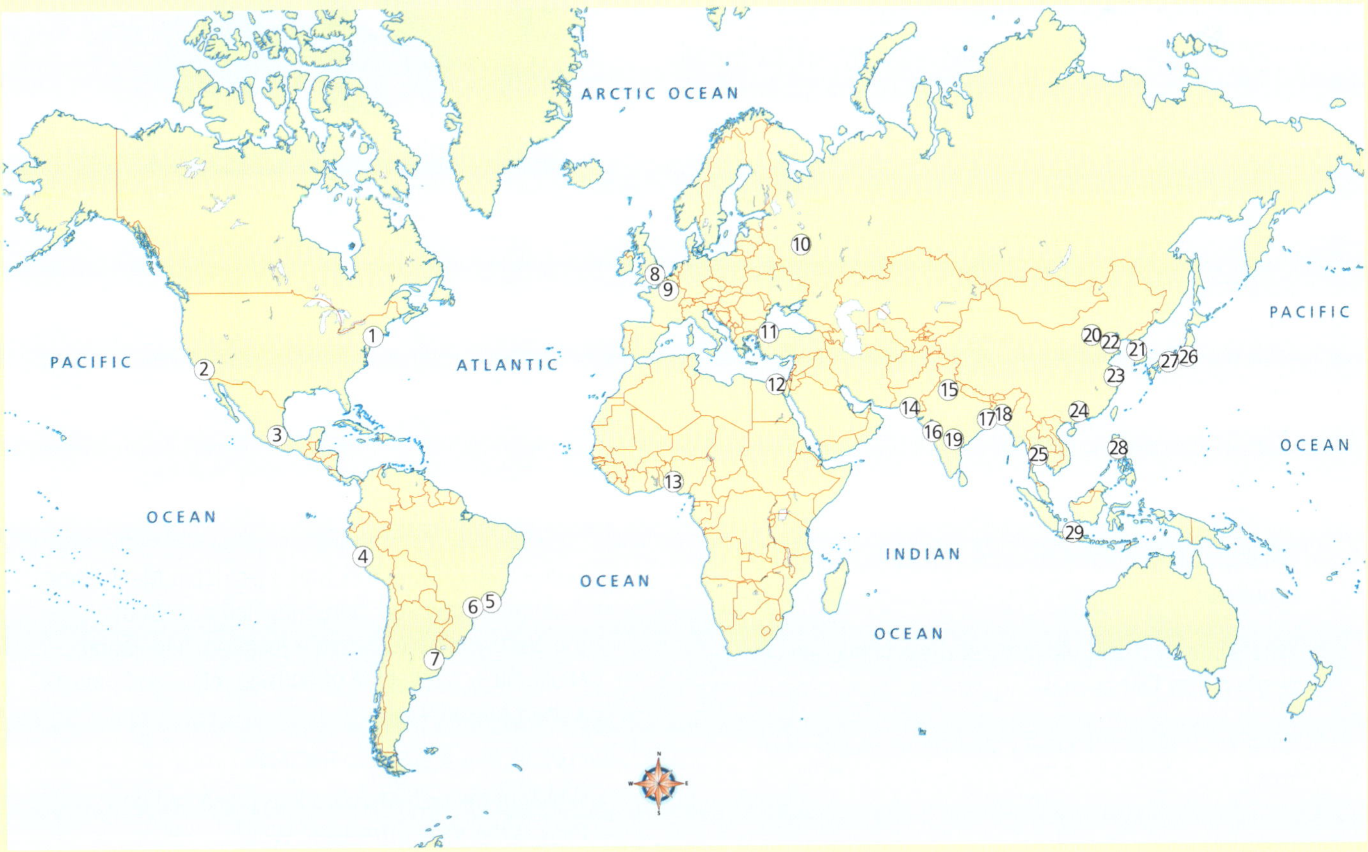

Read and think

FROM HILLS TO SKYSCRAPERS

What the Lenape Native Americans called the 'island of many hills', Manna-hata, could now be called the island of many skyscrapers!

Manhattan originated in the 17th century when the Dutch established a small colony on the island, which they later bought from the Native Americans who inhabited it. New York City had been born! In 1664, the English conquered the colony and called it New York. After the American War of Independence with Great Britain, Manhattan was returned to the United States.

Manhattan experienced considerable growth in the 19th century, as tens of thousands of European immigrants poured into the city, seeking opportunities and religious and political freedom, and attempting to escape poverty and famine. The population of New York rose from around 1 million in 1875 to 3.5 million in 1900, 1.3 million of whom were born in foreign countries.

These immigrants generally lived in dirty, overcrowded tenements in poor neighbourhoods, particularly the Lower East Side. However, jobs were easy to find, although they were often badly-paid, dirty and dangerous. Immigrants were responsible for digging some of the first subway tunnels, building the bridges on the East River and constructing the Flatiron Building, one of first, most emblematic skyscrapers.

The huge increase in the population of New York was one of the reasons why so many skyscrapers were built. Restricted space and the formal grid layout of Manhattan were incentives to build high. New technical developments in buildings and the introduction of lifts made these tall buildings more viable. Moreover, building high is not only a means of maximising the building area, but it also has a prestige value: the higher, the grander!

ANSWER THE QUESTIONS

1. Who were the original inhabitants of the island of Manhattan?
2. Who did they sell the land to?
3. Why did Manhattan grow so much in the 19th century?
4. What problems did the immigrants have in their own countries?
5. What kinds of places did many of these immigrants live in when they first arrived?
6. What kinds of jobs did many immigrants find in New York?
7. What type of urban plan did Manhattan have?
8. Why was it necessary to build upwards?
9. What other advantage does building high have?
10. Investigate and discuss.
    a. Find a map of New York and a district in Manhattan or another New York borough. Find out about the place you have chosen – location, population, economic activity, type of housing, etc – and prepare a short presentation.
    b. Present your findings to the class.
    c. Which of the districts/boroughs presented do you think is the most attractive? Why?

Work it out

CONCEPT MAP

Use the words in the word cloud to create your own unit map in your notebook. Write any connecting texts you need.

megalopolis
conurbation
challenges
supplies
industrial areas
urban waste
types
according to economic activities
working-class neighbourhoods
according to residential area
pollution
metropolitan area
new urban forms
parts
urban areas
world metropolises
social conflict
commercial areas
business areas
transport
urban hierarchy
regional metropolises
national metropolises
housing
small cities
middle-class and upper-class neighbourhoods

SELF-ASSESSMENT

Carry out a self-assessment of what you learnt in this unit. Choose one answer for each question and then check your answers.

1. ... is an area comprising two or more cities that have merged as a result of their growth.
   a. A metropolitan area
   b. A megalopolis
   c. A conurbation
2. ... in Spain took place in the 1960s.
   a. Rural exodus
   b. Growth of rural areas
   c. Population growth
3. New York is an example of a ...
   a. world metropolis.
   b. national metropolis.
   c. regional metropolis.
4. Most Spanish cities can be classified as ...
   a. regional metropolises.
   b. subregional cities.
   c. national metropolises.
5. ... is one of the problems cities face.
   a. Concentration of commercial areas
   b. Pollution
   c. Easily available healthcare
6. The outskirts in a city are bordered by ...
   a. the city centre.
   b. the old town.
   c. peri-urban areas.
7. Huge shantytowns are common in ...
   a. developing countries.
   b. all metropolises.
   c. developed countries.
8. ... is a graphic representation of a space drawn to scale.
   a. An urban drawing
   b. An urban plan
   c. A city aerial photo
9. ... is a place whose inhabitants usually work elsewhere.
   a. An old town
   b. A dormitory town
   c. A commercial area
10. Zaragoza is an example of a ...
   a. national metropolis.
   b. sub-regional city.
   c. regional metropolis.

Big thinkers

Name: Paul-Henri Spaak

Lived: 1899–1972

Nationality: Belgian

Interests: Politics, sports

Bright ideas: Spaak was a very prominent European politician. He believed that uniting countries through treaties was the most effective way of guaranteeing peace and stability in Europe. He was elected president of the first meeting of the United Nations General Assembly and Secretary-General of NATO. He was also a leading figure in creating the content of the Treaty of Rome. He is considered to be one of the greatest contributors to the project of European integration.

Name: Louis Pasteur

Lived: 1822–1895

Nationality: French

Interests: Microbiology, chemistry, medicine, immunology, drawing, painting

Bright ideas: Pasteur is considered to be one of the most important scientists in history. His discoveries have helped to save millions of people. He proved that illnesses were caused by microorganisms. He used this knowledge to develop a process that kills most of the microbes in drinks and foods (pasteurisation). Pasteur also developed vaccines for rabies, chicken cholera and anthrax.

Name: Frank Gehry

Lived: 1929–present day

Nationality: Canadian, American

Interest: Architecture, design, sculpture

Bright ideas: Ghery is considered to be one of the most important modern architects. His best-known works include the Guggenheim Museum in Bilbao, the Walt Disney Concert Hall in Los Angeles and the Dancing House in Prague. In 1989 he was awarded the Pritzker Architecture Prize, sometimes called the Nobel Prize of Architecture.

Glossary

assembly (n): a group of people who gather together to make laws or decisions for a particular country or region

attachment (n): an extra part that can be added to something to perform a particular function

boost (v): to increase or improve something

budget (n): the amount of money available to be spent

contraceptive (n): a method, drug or device used to prevent pregnancy

converge (v): come together from different directions

deploy (v): to move troops or equipment into position for military action

entrepreneurial (adj): taking of financial risk

even out (v): to become equal

foster (v): to encourage the development of something

fulfil (v): to achieve something

guarantee (v): to promise that something will happen

impose (v): to officially force a law, a tax or a punishment

inherit (v): to receive money, titles or property from someone after they have died

malnutrition (n): bad health caused by not eating enough of the right things

merging (n): combining or joining together

overall (adj): taking everything into account

peri-urban (adj): between the suburbs and the countryside

persecute (v): to treat somebody cruelly because of their religion, race or political beliefs

refuge (n): a place or situation that gives protection from danger

regime (n): a type of authoritarian government

repercussion (n): an effect of an action or decision, usually a bad effect

shantytown (n): an area on the outskirts of a city where very poor people live

shortage (n): a situation in which there is not enough of something

shrink (v): to become smaller

skyscraper (n): a very tall building, usually in a city

spike (n): a very high amount or level of something, usually before a fall

spokesperson (n): a person who speaks officially for a group or organisation

swear (v): to take an oath

typhoid fever (n): an infectious disease causing a high temperature, red spots and severe pain in the stomach

veto (v): to refuse to accept